THE ART OF LIVING IN JOY

ARAYEH NOROUZI, PH.D.

PRAISE FOR
THE ART OF LIVING IN JOY

"Dr. Arayeh's *Art of Living in Joy* offers practical tools and tips to live a more joyful, self-determined life. She guides the reader to understand how our fears and beliefs can keep us stuck in detrimental patterns, then teaches us ways to break those patterns and create a more empowered mindset that leads us towards joy." —Dr. Davina Kotulski, Ph.D., Psychologist and Author of *It's Never Too Late to be Your Self and The Manna Paradigm Shift*

"This book might be thought of as a guide for living your life as well as possible. Dr. Arayeh presents a simple but powerful five-step problem-solving tool that can help you find solutions to life's most challenging problems with minimum stress and without suffering. Her tools are backed by an encyclopedia of supporting information, knowledge, and wisdom from many of the world's best minds. Their knowing serves to substantiate and elucidate Dr. Arayeh's recommendations. I highly recommend this book for every human being who presently feels overwhelmed by the explosion of problems related to living in today's modern world." —Dr. Timothy Wilken, M.D.

"This book is incredible! Part memoir, part instructional guide to living an authentic life, this book is a must-read for anyone who is struggling to find deeper meaning, connection, and joy— whether at work, in relationships, or in parenting. Dr. Arayeh draws on multiple philosophical traditions and psychological principles and shares her own life experiences as she walks us through steps to create authentic change in all aspects of our lives and relationships. So much of what she covers resonate deeply with me. It felt like one long, restorative exhale. Give yourself the gift of this engaging, accessible, and transformative book! —Dr. Naseem Badiey, Ph.D. Political Sociologist, Criminal Justice Reform Researcher

"The *Art of Living in Joy* is the handbook I wished we had when growing up. I love how Dr. Arayeh has simplified the steps to living a joyful life. The stories, the examples, everything about this book oozes with love, joy, and immense healing. It's inspiring and motivating all at the same time. There are imperative steps to healing from past wounds and living a fulfilled life in the future. A must-read for everyone in today's troubled times. We all need this manual for a joyful life." —Zeenat Merchant Syal, Counseling Psychologist

"There is so much timeless wisdom packed into this book. The priceless information and genuine inspiration radiate from the pages. *The Art of Living in Joy* is filled with authenticity, vulnerability, sincerity, and so many insights that clarify how to know Joy in the here and now. It's apparent that all Dr. Arayeh has drunk with her thirst for knowledge has become wisdom to now quench the thirst of others." —Gil McIff, Awakening Coach

"This is a practical guide to finding true joy in life with stories that make reading the book enjoyable. It's an inspiring story from an inspiring woman who can quickly help you with proven strategies to live more consciously and joyfully. Dr. Arayeh's P.A.U.S.E. methodology can make any crisis manageable." —Dr. Katty Bidad, M.D., Ph.D., Director of Publishing, *North Star Success Inc.*

"It's rare to find a book that truly captivates everything in an easy-to-read and digestible format—a true gem of a read with one word that continually comes to mind—a masterpiece. If you're searching for truth, in any capacity, and looking or concrete, tried and tested, practical ways to find more joy, peace, and freedom in your life, then you have found it here. Tapping into her life experience, extensive training, research, and life stories, Dr. Arayeh eloquently, compassionately, and poignantly shares her journey. And in so doing will help those who desire and dare to raise their awareness of what it truly takes to harness, capture, and live in joy."—*Louise Clarke, Your Parenting Partner, Author of Parenting the Modern Teen*

"Dr. Arayeh offers a paradigm shift, a way of tapping into our inherent inner joy as a way of navigating life. She shares with readers the events that inspired this book, demonstrating how pain and suffering can be alchemized, yielding pearls of wisdom. Her powerful P.A.U.S.E. method is an in-the-moment tool that can redirect readers, helping them find their way back to their natural state of joy during challenging times." —Dr. Deepti Gandhi, M.D. Physician, Wellness Expert, Public Speaker

"Dr. Arayeh's book is a compelling page-turner filled with road-maps to help us all embrace and understand *"The Art of Living In Joy."* She discusses ways to connect with our inner world, conditioning, generational patterns, etc., to take control of our own lives. Through her thoughtful examples and tangible technics, she provides us with simple methods to living in this higher consciousness, creating more joy." —Sue DeCaro, Worldwide Live and Parent Coach

"I can't recommend Dr. Arayeh enough! She is the true embodiment of the work. Her breadth of knowledge in both psychology and spirituality gives this book the practical edge needed for those who want to deepen our understanding of ourselves, cultivate joy, and embody our Truth!! Thank you for bringing your wisdom to the world at a time we need it the most!" —Goly Emam, Clinical Counsellor, Hypnotherapist

"Dr. Arayeh's warm and wonderful book uses wisdom and humor to help you understand the triggers that stress you out and the tools to help you live in more joy. She vulnerably shares her strengths and her weaknesses which make the book so accessible and real. It was a captivating read from beginning to end, and I've already benefited from the gifts she shared for my joy in my personal and professional life." —Tasia Valenza, Emmy Award winning voiceover artist, Tedx speaker, and founder of *Give Great Voice*

"Powerful and Transformational. This book is packed with practical exercises, making it a workbook. A map, taking you through the steps of acknowledging fear, pain, and suffering within your life to finding true freedom, joy, and love." —Nicole Telfer, Founder of *Empowerd-KidsTV*

"Dr. Arayeh's *Art of Living in Joy* is filled with powerful tools, concepts, and stories that can guide you through the ups and downs of life with elegance and joy. The pearls of wisdom in this book are tremendously accessible to readers through real-life examples that can help people enhance their relationships personally and professionally. Dr. Arayeh's beautiful energy permeates every word she wrote. This book comes with a depth of wisdom dedicated to making the world a better place for all and future generations." —Catherine B. Roy, Personal Growth, and Business Coach, Best-selling Author of *Live From Your Heart and Mind*

"This book is fabulous! Dr. Arayeh helps us live a more connected, conscious, joy-filled life based on her own personal, hardearned wisdom learning how to let go of fear, doubt, and external expectations to live a life that is fulfilling and true to who we are." —Erin Taylor, Business, Parent, Teen, and Life Coach, Author of *Connection & Kindness: The Key to Changing the World Through Parenting*

"Straight from the heart, Dr. Arayeh gives us the comprehensive recipe to transform our pain into the wisdom within our hearts in her book, *The Art of Living in Joy* . The five steps mentioned in the book are an incredible amalgamation of science and practical tools to facilitate healing and thriving relationships, and the journal exercises are an excellent addition. I highly recommend it to anyone looking to turn their pain into abundance."—Kiana Danial, USA Today & WSJ Best-Selling Author, Invest Diva CEO

"An inspired and uplifting work! Dr. Arayeh delights us with a soulful journey to a joyful life. She also makes us a gift by sharing this lucid account of her own personal, transformational journey towards reclaiming joy and becoming an enlightened leader. Read this book. Reflect upon its message and powerful exercises. You'll find yourself with a greater sense and understanding of how to live the remaining days of your life." —Dr. Afsoon Ghazvinian, Wellness Consultant, Women's Health Advocate

"Dr. Arayeh's book is an excellent read for anyone struggling with anxiety or negative thoughts. She provides terrific, practical advice that is easy to follow. Her acronym P.A.U.S.E., which outlines the five recommended steps to rewire your brain, enhances the learning of the sequence and provides quicker recall. I highly recommend this book whether you are a coach working with clients or just want to work on yourself. Well done!" —Dr. Melanie Carr, Ph.D., Author of *Emotional Intelligence for Funeral Directors: The Secret to Less Stress and Burnout at Work*

"This book is an emotional guide to healing. It's a fantastic collection of psychological and spiritual tools and techniques to alleviate suffering and promote healthy emotions. Dr. Arayeh has created a masterpiece by combining ancient spiritual wisdom with modern psychological models of healing and backed up by proven scientific knowledge. We are emotional beings, and our experiences on earth are mainly determined by how we feel in each moment. Dr. Arayeh demonstrates in in this book how we can handle negative the emotions with grace and ease. This book is an encyclopedia of practical exercises for the healing of the mind. This is a must-have for anyone who wants to master how to navigate the emotional lows and highs of life and at the same time, create the life of their dreams." —Dr. Uchenna Ilo, Ph.D., Life Transformation Coach and Researcher

"*The Art of Living in Joy* is like a warm cup of tea by the fire. Conversational, authentic, and methodical, it takes you down a path of self-discovery that will surely benefit all who read Dr. Arayeh's inviting style. I can't wait till it becomes required/recommended reading for high school and college students, as well as the contents for a picture / coloring book for the little ones! Hurrah!" —Judy Julin, CEO & Founder, *WOWLearningLab.com*

"Dr. Arayeh truly is an inspiration to many. This book is filled with great insights on how she's taken strides to overcome challenges and excelled beyond barriers from the country, heritage, and language to be where she is today! The tools she provides in the book are powerful for the readers to follow and implement." —Liza Boubari, Certified Clinical Hypnotherapist

"Wow, wow, wow, I love The Art of Living in Joy . Dr. Arayeh shares her wisdom so eloquently in this book. Each chapter is full of thought-provoking insights which deeply resonate with me. Dr. Arayeh's heart-centered guidance has empowered me to implement the practical steps into my life and feel more connected, fulfilled, and joyful." —Sarah Willoughby, Transformation Coach, Author of *Infertility Saved My Life*

"Dr. Arayeh's book offered simple yet highly effective practical ideas and suggestions that can be applied right away in your daily life, (to be more present and reconnect to our birthright of joy.) It's a must-read for all, especially anyone that wants to learn how to deepen their spiritual practice." —Dr. Chanie Messinger, Coach, OTR/L, AAPC, ABNLP, Author

"A brilliant work of spiritual and psychological wisdom that moves the reader to healing and joy! Dr. Arayeh imparts personal stories on her path to awakening and shares current and ancient insights from spiritual giants." —Coleen Gsell, Executive Director of Center for Spiritual Awakening

"I believe they are no bad people, just people in pain. Dr. Arayeh helps us understand the root cause of our pain; she gives practical steps with efficient tools to end the suffering and focus on the joy of living." —Dr. Taggy Bensaid, ND

"Dr. Arayeh has spent years studying human psychology and developing effective ways to create transformation in the quality of people's lives and their relationships. Her book offers a wealth of information that anyone from any walk of life and in any field of work can greatly benefit from." —Raeeka Yaghmai, Dating & Relationship Coach

"Reading *The Art of Living In Joy*, I see a decade's worth of research and application taking all of the best concepts personal development offers, consolidating them into one poignant novel. Though the book can help anyone who reads it, it was especially applicable to me as a parent of three small children. Dr. Arayeh describes her children as her teachers and radical awakeners, and I couldn't agree more. This book contains how to go from just parenting to becoming mindful in every interaction with our kids, which is a powerful reminder to me. With a Ph.D. in psychology, certifications in several modalities of coaching, and a frequent lecturer and speaker for parenting workshops and individuals, she is an expert on the subject of Joy. I am excited for you, the reader, on the journey you are about to take as you delve into these pages. Enjoy! But most importantly, read them in joy." —Madeline Bracken, MBA, High-Performance Coach

"The Art of Living in Joy is a delightful guide full of important information for anyone who needs a roadmap to freedom and a joyful life with full awareness. I commend Dr. Arayeh's courage and willingness to share her experience throughout her journey to become a person who can help and bring peace and joy to others. This book is an excellent contribution to deepening our understanding of what it means to be human." —Dr. Yassamin Ilyavi, Ph.D., MBA, Corporate Wellness Consultant

"*The Art of Living in Joy* is not just an inspiring story of resilience and hope. This book also offers the guidance to help us understand how to connect with ourselves so that we can ensure our mind, body, and spirit are balanced and live from a place of pure Joy!" —Barbara Vercruysse, Global Kindness Advocate, CEO & Founder of *BV Empowerment & Kindness Institute*, #1 Top 50 Global Thought Leaders on Mental Health

"To be able to talk about joy, write about joy, find a clear path to get to joy, one must truly deeply live and embody it. I have not come across any other that has been able to put into words a fully practical way of doing this other than Dr. Arayeh. This book is a true gift to all. I wish for any and all, ready to receive such wisdom and joy, to do so with this book." —Dinuka Ranasinghe, Conscious Living and Parenting Coach, Attorney

"After reading *The Art of Living in Joy,* I was in awe. I sat and began to reflect on my life and my decisions in life. I realized that we must always start from within and dig deep to make decisions and not act on impulses. In life, we are always trying to make others happy and often forget about ourselves. I will take your life experiences and ponder how I can make future decisions by pausing and breathing." —Dr. Tonia Barnes, EdD, Organizational Leadership

"Dr. Arayeh has beautifully woven scientific facts with heart-based practices to create a roadmap to living a joyful life. She takes the readers on a journey, giving glimpses of her personal life by sharing anecdotes that make the book very relatable and inspiring. Conratulations, Dr. Arayeh, for writing this amazing book that can be used as a support tool for anyone who wishes to live their best life." —Bhavya Gaur, Soulful Empowerment & Transformation Coach, International Bestselling Author

THE ART OF LIVING IN JOY

Five Practical Steps to Transform
Life Challenges into Joy and Harmony

ARAYEH NOROUZI, PH.D.

PDF SUMMARY

I've created a PDF summary going over the system I cover in this book for faster brain reprogramming. You can download it here:

coaching.drarayeh.com/joyful-living

Dedication

This book is dedicated to my beloved husband, children, and parents. Thank you for saying "yes" to my dream.

Acknowledgement

First, I would like to express my ever-increasing gratitude for the divine for empowering me and awakening me to my higher purpose. I would also like to acknowledge my coach, Gil McIff, who got me started on my awakening journey, and my mentor Dr. Shefali Tsabary who enlightened me, emboldened me, and inspired me to unshackle from my conditioning and step into my authentic essence, passion, and purpose. Thank you both for offering me a different worldview that is free from suffering, bondage, and scarcity.

I would also like to mention the names of many Eastern and Western teachers and guides, alive or in spirit, who have been a bright light on my path of this intricate journey called life: Persian poets and mystics such as Jalāl al-Dīn Muammad Rūmī (Rumi), Hafiz, Khayyam, Attar, Sohrab Sepehri; Eastern guides such as Siddhartha Gautama (Buddha), Lao Tzu, Thich Nhat Hanh, Yongey Mingyur Rinpoche, Nichiren Daishonin, Gurumai Chidvilasananda, Swami Muktananda, Paramahansa Yogananda, Ramana Maharishi, Maharishi Mahesh Yogi, Dalai Lama, and Sadhguru; and those who live(d) in the West, Albert Einstein, Carl Jung, William James, Viktor E. Frankl, Ken Wilber, Jon Kabat-Zinn, Dr. Gabor Maté, Dr. Deepak Chopra, Dr. Joe Dispenza, Dr. Bruce Lipton, Dr. Daniel J. Siegel, Byron Katie, Eckhart Tolle, Neale Donald Walsch, Louise Hay, Dr. Joe Vitale, Napoleon Hill, Tony Robbins, Sonia Choquette, Christie Marie Sheldon, Donna Eden, and Dr. Bill Little.

Rumi, the 13th-century Persian poet, scholar, and esteemed Sufi mystic, said, "What you seek is seeking you." All my life, I have been seeking divine truth and dreaming of ways I could cultivate and embody peace and joy in my life to serve my fellow humans in meaningful and tangible ways. I know in my heart that writing this book is a grand step toward this dream.

I also know that my soul sought and found a partner in life that made some of these dreams come true, without whom I would have never written these words. I sincerely thank my husband, Farzin, who has been the embodiment of love, support, and companionship, empowering me in my personal, educational, and professional journey over the past years. I also wholeheartedly thank my parents for believing in me and prioritizing me all their lives so I could achieve my far-fetched goals and dreams.

Lastly, I thank my beloved children, my teachers and my radical awakeners, Mauna and Nima, who have blessed my life with their presence and endured my occasional absence as I traversed my multi-faceted life journeys. Thank you for showing up in my life and being who you are so I can understand who I am. Thank you for loving me when I was not so lovable and for forgiving me when I could not forgive myself.

It's my hope that I have also taught you to make conscious efforts toward your dreams. I am thrilled that you are awakening to the fact that you are inherently enough, believe you have all the answers within you, knowing that your outer world is a reflection of your inner world, and trusting you can achieve anything you can imagine.

CONTENTS

Introduction

In the first two chapters of this book, I prepare the reader for a methodical five-step formula, P.A.U.S.E. This helps to rewire the brain from fear to love, suffering to joy, and dependency to freedom. In the last chapter, I dive deeper into the human condition and our place in the cosmos.

Throughout the book, you will find real-life examples, descriptive illustrations, journal entries, practical exercises, and further recommended resources to facilitate deeper, faster, and more effective brain reprogramming. Furthermore, you may come across sections about the way a child's brain develops. Even if you might not have a child of your own, it's essential to read through those sections since we all have a child within us, our inner child who frequently reacts whenever something triggers us emotionally.

As you read this book, think of yourself having hired a personal life coach who is always there when you need her!

P.A.U.S.E. offers you a comprehensive, step-by-step system that gives you a practical pathway to the *Art of Living in Joy* because you deserve to feel good, abundant, and free. I believe joy is our birthright and, I feel honored that we're going on a journey together to claim it.

CHAPTER ONE
THE HERO'S JOURNEY
THE PAIN TOO GRAVE, THE SHELL TOO CONFINING

The Journey Begins

A group of individuals have lived their whole lives chained to the wall in a cave. For them, their world consists of shadows that are projected on the wall they are facing. In his allegory of the cave, the Greek philosopher Plato describes how a thinker who was a former prisoner has been liberated. Now he can see the actual reality of the world.

I was a prisoner of the Cave.

In the year 1996, I began my journey toward liberation. A group of close friends and family gathered in our house to see me off at the airport. I had given away all my cherished belongings and was bidding farewell to my beloved room, my parents, my aunts and uncles, my cousins, my friends, and my country.

I left behind all that was familiar to me, and yet unfamiliar to the depth of my soul. I was ready to embark on reconciling my body, mind, and spirit. I was stepping into the unknown in hopes of finding the peace and joy I longed for.

Born in Iran, I had lived and breathed the poem of my beloved Persian poet, Rumi, for many years:

Whoever brought me here

All day I think about it, then at night I say it.
Where did I come from,
And what am I supposed to be doing?
I have no idea.
My soul is from elsewhere, I'm sure of that,
And I intend to end up there. – Rumi[1]

It was time to find answers.

The plane was taking off. My head scarf and uniform were drenched in tears. It was the first time that I was hit by a colossal dose of reality. I was actually leaving the country without a specific plan.

Except for the one month that I was stuck in Ankara, Turkey due to the closure of the American Embassy, where I was trying to obtain my U.S. student visa and was rejected, I had never spent a night away from my parents. As the tears rolled onto my lap, they burned my face.

Looking out of the plane window, I tried to make sense of the moment. Since the evening before, it seemed as if I was intoxicated. Had I stepped into another dimension?

As we took off from the only familiar soil I had known, I realized I was leaving my home and heading towards homelessness. I never thought of it that way until then.

When the plane landed on my first stop in East Asia, I felt empty, unprotected, and vulnerable. This was the first time I almost regretted my decision. I wished I could return home. I was alone, cold, and a bitterness filled my soul.

As I sat down to fill out paperwork, a middle-aged pale Iranian lady wrapped in a scarf just like me noticed my rolling tears and asked, "What's wrong my daughter?"

I sobbed, "I fled my home for a better place and now I'm almost regretful of my decision. I feel an empty hole in place of my heart. I'm lonely and scared. I wish I could hold my parents and tell them how much I need them and how I miss them."

---

1   Translated by Coleman Barks

She stroked me and talked to me like a mother from a perfect dream. She comforted me with her maternal demeanor and assured me I was doing the right thing. She told me how her son had also made a similar decision several years ago to go to New Zealand and how happy he was with his life now. She radiated confidence.

That was it. Her words dissolved any remaining distrust in my decision to leave. Never again did I feel any trace of doubt about the life-altering choice I had made. I had left the Cave and began my Hero's Journey.[2]

In the past several decades I have moved many times from continent to continent, country to country, and city to city. During seven of those moves, I had to sell all my belongings and start over. I knew in the depths of my being that I had to be torn from the home I was born into to realize a couple of decades later that the home I have returned to isn't located in the East or the West.

It took an upward spiral of leaving home and coming back to it over and over before I realized that my home dwells *within my own heart*.

Have You Checked the Boxes?

I grew to be an independent-thinker but inadvertently became the subject of social conformity in all areas of life. I got married like everyone else, was divorced like half the people, married again similar to many, had two kids like many families, earned my degrees, found a job in the corporate world, saved money to buy a house, and went on vacations once in a while because I needed a break from life just like everyone else.

Education-wise, as an adolescent in Persian culture, I had two choices—to become a doctor or an engineer. I hated the sight of blood, so I chose physics and mathematics as my high school major. Some of the formal education I was somehow pressed to embark upon were bachelor's programs in applied physics, and

---

2   Hero's Journey, popularized by Joseph Campbell, is a common story plot involving a hero who goes on a journey and returns home transformed.

English translation in Tehran, and computer science, followed by a master's degree in computer and electrical engineering in Toronto, Canada. Even when I landed in the land of the free, I was influenced by the dot-com wave and chose computer science instead of astronomy, although this had been my passion for years.

It was not until I had checked all the boxes that I was called to come to a screeching halt and literally pause.

When I resigned from my corporate e-commerce development job, I knew it was time to reevaluate all my choices. I needed time to tear off my masks and unshackle myself from the variety of chains I had grown to live with.

Serendipitously, I awakened to the fact that I had been consciously or unconsciously coerced into making all my life decisions. I either did it because my status-craving culture expected me to conform, world financial circumstances dictated my educational decisions, or simply because I was made to believe I had to subserviently follow an illusory life itinerary like everyone else or I would fail as an individual

Now that I look at the trajectory of my life up until that point, it seems like it was more of a rat race than a living.

I had never consciously thought about this before the inspired pause. I never once stopped to think about the fact that we're human beings, not human doings. I believed I would not be worthy if I left any of these boxes unchecked. However, even checking all of them failed to lead to nourishing my hungry soul. I craved to know who brought me here, where I came from, and what I was supposed to be doing with my life.

It makes complete sense to me when Jim Carrey, the world-famous Canadian-American actor, says, "I think everybody should get rich and famous and do everything they ever dreamed of so they can see that it's not the answer."

If the slightest thing didn't go my way in my personal and professional life, feelings of failure surged up. Truly, every failure felt like a death.

I wish I knew what I know now, that this was simply my fight-flight-freeze brain treating a simple bump as a life-or-death situation.

I wish I knew that feelings, thoughts, and life's events are like waves of the ocean that come and go, but never stay.

I wish I could have fathomed that life by nature is volatile, unpredictable, and impermanent...and as the Buddhists say, "the glass is already broken."

I knew the roadmap was missing. I was lost, but I was inspired enough to stop and acknowledge this. Part of that acknowledgement was that desk work wasn't what I was designed to do forever.

So, I paused.

Empty Your Cup

Once upon a time, a wise Zen master offered his wisdom to those who asked for a path to enlightenment.

One day a conceited scholar came to him to ask for advice. Soon the Zen master observed how the man was already biased with his own opinion and judgments and not ready to receive new knowledge.

To teach him a lesson, he said that they should discuss the matter over a cup of tea. He started pouring tea into his teacup and didn't stop even when the cup overflowed onto the table and on the scholar's robe. The scholar angrily yelled, "Stop! Can't you see the cup is already full?"

The Zen master replied, "Exactly! You are like this cup, so full of beliefs and ideas that nothing more can fit in. Come back when your cup is empty. Come back to me with an open mind."

It was not until my resignation from my corporate job that I was auspiciously awakened to the fact that I had been living like a robot. I knew what I didn't want to do, but I had no idea what I wanted to do. I just knew how I wanted to *feel*.

That is how I became an empty cup. I released all my assumptions, beliefs, speculations, shoulds and shouldn'ts. Instead, I asked my deeper self to inspire me with the answer.

Ask and It Is Given

I was truly curious to know how people perceived me. Were they able to pinpoint my calling from their perspective?

In the meantime, I launched into a journey of soul-searching, along with researching about the human condition, brain programming, the power of the subconscious mind, the impact of childhood conditioning, quantum science, and the power of the heart. After exactly one month, I received the response I had been seeking.

I became a certified life coach from a company I had received services from as a result of my research. I not only chose to forego a substantial monthly income from a 9-5 job, but I began heavily investing in my personal development and business ventures with the hope that it would pay off.

Little did I know, I was unable to be self-employed since I was living in the United States with a Canadian work visa. Not being able to legally work, I persuaded my family for yet another grand decision to go for my Ph.D. in psychology.

Sometimes people tell me that not everyone can do what I did because they might not have an agreeable circumstance as I did. I say to them, "The circumstances were so because I was adamant to take the leap, not the other way around."

Our inner longings would not be there if we could not attain them. Once we have a heartfelt desire, it means we already have the potential to fulfill it. There is a reason for our innate aspirations, and it is our duty to honor them and jump without overthinking the *how*.

The Universe Is a Yes Machine

I've long pondered a statement of Albert Einstein, one of the greatest and most influential physicists of all time: "The most important decision we make is whether we believe we live in a friendly or hostile universe."

If this is the case, it means we co-create our world based on our deepest feelings. As I thought about this, it seemed to me that the world we live in is either neutral toward us or possibly a *yes* machine. Could it be that instead of being against us, as some believe, it says yes to our deepest beliefs and yearnings?

What if the opposite was the case, that it also says yes to our fears?

It's crucial to examine our deep-seated conditioning. I began to notice that when fear dictated my decisions, they were never fulfilling. At times I even manifested the things I feared most.

It seemed to me that my outer world so often became a reflection of my thoughts and emotions. I noticed that when I start a day on a good note, I often experience a joyful day. On the other hand, I tended to experience a series of nasty mishaps if I happened to get out of bed on a wrong side.

At any moment in time, a myriad of things could go wrong, whether in our body, our family, at work, with our finances, or as a result of an accident or a natural disaster. But we forget that and take all the "right" things for granted. Our ego defense mechanism that was predetermined in childhood like the rest of our conditioning, is programmed to focus on the "wrong" things no matter how trivial they are in order to keep us safe. To put it in a nutshell, our brain has a bias towards negativity.

Furthermore, the ego's naïve mechanism that constantly monitors our environment for possible threats believes it's actually doing something tangible by making us continually worried.

Becoming cognizant of this mental dynamic can bring great awareness to our internal state. This is important because our state of mind is what our inner being wants us to say *yes* to most all the time.

Life is a mirror and reflects back to us what we think and feel. Most of our thinking is unconscious, and we're not even aware of it much of the time. It can be hard to dramatically shift the way we think. Nevertheless, we can at least focus on emptying our cup while releasing our fearful stories. We then become receptive, curious, and open to fresh ideas.

After I resigned from my last job, this is what I felt I needed to do. I became an empty cup!

Because I frequently complained about my reactivity toward my children, my coach in the program introduced me to Dr. Shefali Tsabary, clinical psychologist, best-selling author, and Oprah Winfrey's favorite parenting expert. I learned that Carl Jung, the founder of analytical psychology, said that "Everything that irritates us about others can lead us to an understanding of ourselves." As I embarked on conscious living by looking into Dr. Shefali's conscious parenting style, my coach sensed I would be inspired to further deconstruct my triggers—and so my awakening journey began.

The Universe said yes to me when I was craving the Truth and quenched my thirst. The Universe said yes to me when I trusted it and endowed me with a trustworthy and tender worldview. The Universe said yes to me when I emptied my cup. I decided to believe this is a *friendly Universe*. And this is the world I chose to dwell in since then.

"What You Seek Is Seeking You." —Rumi

I was in awe of how my eight-year-old daughter's sullen face, which was impregnated with hurt and childhood wounds, had magically turned into a loving and carefree impression in a flash.

I had just learned that there was a powerful electromagnetic field with a proximity of several feet around our hearts that can affect the people and things around us. Having an analytical mind, I ventured to test this. That was the moment I witnessed the transcendent power of my heart on my life and the lives of my loved ones.

On that day, similar to other days, my daughter had greeted me with a surly expression on her face and a harsh comment right aft-ter she had returned from school. However, I decided to overlook my agony and the need to correct her unkind language. To cultivate love in my heart for testing purposes, without trying to put a smile on my face, I intended to remember the beautiful memory of the first night she was born. I had not slept for the whole night on the day she was born so I could fully absorb the weight of her precious body on my bare chest. The scrumptious memory quickly inundated my heart with admiration, gratitude, and reverence.

I was standing about a meter away from her, and before a second passed, I noticed the positive shift on her face. I was flabbergasted. How could it be? How could a mere positive feeling in my heart affect a person's feeling a meter away from me?

That was the instant I felt empowered for the first time as a mother. I discovered something within me beyond my instinctual need to control and my automatic fear-based thoughts and emotions. I started diving deep into my essence that yearned to live with intention and awareness. I recognized that I had a choice. I was not helpless. I had all I needed including compassion, understanding, and the power of presence.

My daughter was two years and three months when my son was born. Being an only child, I had no clue how to deal with her sibling rivalry. That was the time I read around a hundred parenting books, went to all the parenting workshops, had parent coaches come to my house, and even asked my family doctor to medicate me so I wouldn't get triggered with my kids when they failed to fulfill my intention of being the "perfect mother." I even took the "vow of yellibacy," vowing not to yell – as Dr. Laura Markham, a clinical psychologist and the author of *Peaceful Parents, Happy Kids*, advises. All the tools worked, but only for a few days. Then it was like someone hit the reset button back to my children's bickering and jealousy, and my own frustration, impulsive reactivity, and guilty feelings.

When I resigned from my corporate job, the inner knowing that my occupation had to be beyond a pay-the-bills machine, intertwined with easing my parenting struggle, catapulted me into a path of awakening. I learned how we regurgitate the psychological conditioning implanted in us by our caregivers during childhood. I realized we very well could be the prisoners of Plato's Cave.

I was amazed how almost every infinitesimal action, every thought we consciously or unconsciously think, and every feeling we feel is done in an automatic and impulsive manner. I learned how our thoughts lead to our feelings and how our feelings have the power to make our reality. I noticed my daughter's demeanor was directly interconnected with my feelings, but also that my entire world was at the mercy of my awareness. I experienced the reality that "like attracts like." If I wanted to attract bliss, I had first better cultivate the feeling.

All the knowledge I obtained amazed me, awakened me, and most significantly emboldened me to rise above my involuntary driven patterns. This was my calling—learning and teaching how to cultivate awareness of our authentic and limitless self from our fear-thinking and past programming. I had found the deep-seated wisdom that was buried in me all along. This was why the knowledge I was gobbling up from various sources felt true to my soul.

All the teachers I was learning from were tapping into the same pool of wisdom that I also had access to. They were all helping me to wake up from a lifelong amnesia. I saw how my inner light yearned to shine regardless of judgments and expectations. I felt in the cells of my body that I was whole and untouchable on the inside regardless of the times I felt broken, incomplete, and unworthy on the outside.

Although I suddenly uncovered the hidden treasures in my heart, I also had science to back me up and appease my rational mind with scientific yet magical gems. I learned that we can scientifically alter our way of behaving and rewire our neural pathways because of a phenomenon called brain neuroplasticity. I understood how our way of observing the world can tangibly influence our experiences according to quantum science.

I was enthralled that our thoughts directly influence our immune system according to the science of psychoimmunology. I was amazed to find that according to the science of epigenetics, we're not even bound to our genes as it used to be believed. The function of our genes is modulated by the environment, meaning they can be switched on and off by our environmental, physical, mental, and emotional state.

This empowered me to take a colossal leap and release the sabotaging belief that I would never be able to stop yelling at my kids because I was the carrier of a paternal gene of anger and reactivity. Now, I knew why I couldn't keep my vow of *yellibacy.* It was partly because I subconsciously believed I couldn't and partly because of my childhood wounds, past conditioning, and upbringing. It was like I was trying to row a boat not knowing the boat was kept in its place by an anchor. I suddenly realized that I simply had to lift the anchor before rowing.

There was no turning back. My love for truth was so fervent that I began fusing science with heart-based practices to create a roadmap to living in joy, freedom, and peace of mind for myself and those whose lives I am privileged to touch. While I was seeking for the truth, I had no idea that the truth was seeking me. I just needed to empty my cup for my desires to manifest themselves with elegance and grace.

CHAPTER 2

HOPE FOR A TREASURE

The Secret You Want to Know is in the Ebb and Flow

What propelled me to keep digging was that I assumed there must be an enchanted potion, a mystical mantra, or a carefully hidden formula out there that could magically save me and my human fellows from agony, overwhelm, scarcity, and resentment.

The more I dug, the more I saw this was nothing but an illusion. In order for the human experience to make sense, we need the dark and the light, the ebb and the flow, the pain and the ease, the contraction and the expansion, the bitter and the sweet. One simply cannot exist without the other. The trick is to be cognizant of the unity underlying the façade of this polarity, to transcend the transient and theatrical nature of life, not to identify with our experiences, and to know that this too shall pass, as the Sufis say.

Our brain erroneously believes all life events are permanent when we're in the midst of them. It's tremendously challenging to detach from the gravity of the situation unless we have actively done some serious inner work. We feel attacked and sometimes paralyzed by the rush of unprocessed thoughts and feelings. We feel like a defeated victim as if there is no way out of the current predicament. We sit at the center of a circle formed by all the things that are going "wrong."

Our dexterous mind makes us remember and focus on every shortage, failure, and heartbreak we might be experiencing in all aspects of our life. If we were willing, we could list thousands, if not millions of things that are going "right" at any point in time.

We're not having a heart attack or stroke. We're not suffering from unbearable pain. All our organs and the 37.2 trillion cells in our body function to keep us alive, and for the most part healthy. We're safe. Most of the time there are no imminent fires, hurricanes, earthquakes, or floods. We have a place to live, food to eat, and air to breathe. Last but not least, we're not hiding in the basement of our home in the dark because the radio announced a red alarm for a possible aerial missile attack from a neighboring country—yes, I can be very specific about this experience since I have lived through it many times in my childhood back home.

The question is why our mind cannot focus on all the things that go "right" and instead chooses to aggravate us with a perception of one thing that goes "wrong"?

As much as this mechanism seems irritating, it was instilled in our brain to protect us and help us survive our childhood. I found that the best strategy is to converse with this part of the brain, thank it, and retire it by engaging in conscious rationalization or reframing.

We can tell whether a fear is just that—a fear about a possible event that might not even manifest or has a low probability of doing so. In case something has already gone "wrong," this aspect of our psyche can remind ourselves that the problem is not here to stay. To this day, have we not survived every heartbreak, every struggle, and all the quandaries of our life? We're resilient beyond words, but we keep forgetting this.

Like events, feelings are also transient. Children are experts at this. One moment they cry like there is no tomorrow, and the next moment they are laughing as if nothing occurred. They are a perfect model for us. Children are unapologetically in touch with their feelings and process them as they arise in whatever way is needed. This is the case until we adult care-givers attempt to disrupt this process by applying a punishment-and-reward system to make them stop and suppress their feelings because their nagging, crying, and screaming make us uncomfortable.

Feelings are like the waves of the ocean. They are transient. They never stay, and the more we pay attention to them, the faster they dissolve. Research shows that the duration of a feeling does not exceed a couple of minutes. The trick is to feel the feeling in our body and not to ruminate on the story we tell ourselves. Each feeling arises because it has a messenger we need to pay attention to. Then it leaves when its mission is complete.

Anger might want to convey that we need more self-care, stronger boundaries, or a radical shift in our perspective. We must feel our feelings and pay attention to them to heal them. Only then are we liberated from the chains of suppressed emotion. For example, by not properly attending to the healthy feeling of anger over a period of time, after a period of dormancy, we might finally rage like an erupting volcano.[3]

When we accept the fleeting nature of life, we stop resisting the as-is of life. We are no longer at the mercy of someone or something to make us feel happy, content, or at peace. This is how we release the need to control life since we know control is an illusion. Because we are free from expectations, we are no longer disappointed. We take the moments as they come and release them as they leave.

The secret is that there are no secrets to having an ever rosy, bubbly life—and honestly, we do not want that. Life is a play with many acts, and we must become skilled and detached observers if we want to truly enjoy it. Begrudging the scenes, abhorring the actors, and resisting the plots can only bring us misery.

Wanting to always feel upbeat, never getting overwhelmed, and not ever experiencing hardship only creates resentment about our current experience and severs us from living in authenticity and flow. It also makes life boring and uneventful.

---

3   Emotional literacy will be extensively discussed in the second step of the P.A.U.S.E.

We are the witness of our human experiences and need to observe them without judgment, expectation, and a need to control. This doesn't mean that we don't act upon injustice or conform and become unmotivated. It means we preserve our life force that could be otherwise wasted by resenting and resisting the as-is, using it instead to set healthy boundaries and take inspired and compassionate actions for the advancement of our soul.

Worrying Is a Waste of Resources

"If you believe that feeling bad or worrying long enough will change a past or future event, then you are residing on another planet with a different reality system."
—William James

The defense mechanism of our brain is predisposed to keeping us worried and on the edge almost all the time. It naïvely presumes worrying accomplishes something. While we can use our imagination and visualization capabilities to intentionally co-create an abundant and pleasant life in the present moment, we waste these resources when we fabricate worst-case scenarios or wallow in past events.

Is this not an abuse of our mental skills? Is it not true that the past is gone and the future has not yet arrived? Most of our worries are illusions, mere stories in our mind. Nevertheless, we constantly immerse ourselves in the thoughts related to the past and future.

Once we know this is how our mind operates, it's easy to trace the thoughts that worry us, overwhelm us, or infuriate us. Let me illustrate two factors that contribute to our frustration.

One morning my son had a hard time keeping up with distance-learning. I could easily have paused my work and spent a few minutes attending to him by making him feel seen and safe, possibly helping him problem-solve. Instead, I chose to unconsciously plot a scenario in my head about a dire future in which he would never be able to do his work independently and I would need to spoon-feed him forever.

I was provoked since the situation made me feel out of control myself. My own tasks were overwhelming me, and I was feeling helpless about my condition. My son's curriculum situation was an added stress. I had projected my deeply-ingrained feelings of powerlessness onto him, a situation that could have easily been mitigated if I hadn't unconsciously read too much into it. Furthermore, how could I have recognized the feeling of helplessness if I hadn't repeatedly experienced it in the past? The experience with my son had triggered a similar memory in my childhood from when I felt out-of-control and at the mercy of my parents' judgments.

One factor that contributes to our agony operates in the past and is activated as a result of a childhood experience. The other factor operates in the future because of a fear-based speculation, neither related to the present moment. Had I been able to be cognizant of this duo at that moment, I could have released it and adopted a more conscious and compassion-based approach instead of reacting and perpetuating a power struggle between myself and my son.

By letting fears of the future and the pains of the past interfere with the present moment, we regurgitate our emotional and behavioral patterns. This prevents us from having fresh and creative perspectives, which means we don't think outside the box. Instead, we perpetuate the habit of disconnecting from the present by pulling files out of the cabinet in our brain to match the current experiences with a memory from the past. This upholds a vicious cycle until we decide to interrupt the pattern and consciously make a different choice.

No Mud, No Lotus

Last year I was a "victim" of a scam call and lost $14,000. These skilled individuals usually employ fear or greed to entrap people. I was the victim of fear. Over ten hours a group of four people used legitimate government official names and phone numbers to throw legal terms and threatening language at me, successfully paralyzing my connection to my inner knowing.

The so-called police officer said I had been served a subpoena to be a witness in one of my clients' court sessions, signed it, but never appeared in court. When I said I never signed such a form, they said it was no problem and I could go to the police station and verify my signature. When I agreed to go, they said I would be arrested if I stepped in the station and therefore needed to set a refundable bond before entering the premises.

When I wanted to talk to my family members, they said there was a gag order on and I should not discuss it in public. They even told me I should Google gag order to understand the meaning. To my panicky mind, everything they said made sense. I even Googled the government official names and numbers. They were all legitimate. I had no idea people could spoof a specific contact number that appears on a caller ID.

Although I was traumatized, because of what I teach, not even for a second did I become trapped in a victim mentality. Instead of complaining *why* this happened to me, I kept asking *what* treasure my soul wanted me to dig out from the ruins. Because I asked the right question from the universe, I received gems as answers.

The first and immediate lesson I learned was that there are not many legitimate emergencies out there unless there is one, of course. If your child is jumping into traffic, please do not wait and take deep breaths or count from five to one. However, how many real emergencies can we name, and what is their proportion to all other cases we erroneously and frequently assume are valid urgent scenarios?

There are very few circumstances that need our urgent and speedy reaction. When driving, we can always pull off the road and attend to our children's needs in the back seat instead of choosing to yell while driving. Even if we're driving to the airport and miss our flight, our losses can still be compensated. And we can always delay getting our point across with our partners, children, friends, or colleagues.

There barely exists a real danger when it comes to relationships, but we unconsciously feel threatened and choose to "fight to be right." I always knew I needed to stay more composed in the heat of the moment, but what better life experience could more effectively and unequivocally help me embody this concept? Yes, it was an insanely traumatizing incident, and I lost a great deal of money, but I am grateful that these were all repairable losses accompanied by pearls of wisdom.

Being of service to my fellow humans in a meaningful way and genuinely enjoying my day-to-day work were some of the reasons I changed my career. Up until the scamming incident, the pressure of building a business from the ground up had unequivocally misplaced my vision of service on the back burner. This felt inevitable since I had to be the writer, the designer, the course creator, the content creator, the tech person, the market researcher, the bookkeeper, and the social media expert all in one.

Furthermore, I had to facilitate distance learning for my kids, entertain them so they did not want to always engage in screening, which I wholeheartedly despised, and balance family responsibilities, work, exercise, and meditation time as much as I could.

The busyness of my daily work had prevented me from maintaining my vision close to my heart and embodying gratitude and joy in the process. I was so focused on how to accomplish the next task, find the next client, and create the next content that I had forgotten to be grateful for what I already had. Although I spent a couple of hours meditating, exercising, spending time in nature, and experiencing peace every morning, I was so absorbed in the thick of daily work that it had turned into another J.O.B.

I had grown to neglect reveling in the nectar of the present moment, enjoying my relationships, and celebrating my professional triumphs on a moment-by-moment basis. I had been ignoring the Art of Living in Joy! This realization was only revealed after I had ceaselessly and religiously asked for it for many weeks after the scamming incident. But the value was undeniably in the wait.

They say, "People that pay, pay attention!" I had definitely paid and certainly paid attention.

Until we can fully cultivate gratitude for having $300 in our bank account, we will not be able to manifest $300,000. Even if we do, there is little chance that we know how to be grateful for it.

Joy is a mental state that can be embodied without an iota of influence from the outside. Joy is a decision, an inside job. It felt like I had hit the jackpot of joyful living by learning to cherish the abundance in the here and now. How could I fully grasp this teaching if I had not lived it in my body through the muddy and murky experience of being scammed?

A natural pearl develops when an irritant, often a parasite, gets trapped in a particular species of an oyster, mussel, or clam. When the defense mechanism of the mollusk secretes a fluid to cover the irritant over and over, a luminous pearl is formed. This is how we develop our pearls of wisdom. An irritant in life is just that, an irritant, but it can alchemically transform into the gems of insight through our zeal, grit, and reflection.

The trick is to be a nonjudgmental recipient and not get hardened or duped by the façade of the adversities of life. Just like the lotus flower has its roots in the dirtiest waters, we can also rise and bloom in the hardest of circumstances and flourish to our fulfilled and graceful essence.

Thich Nhat Hanh, Vietnamese Buddhist teacher and peace activist said, "A lotus can never grow without mud. We cannot plant a lotus on marble. So just as the mud plays a very vital role in bringing out the lotus, suffering plays a vital role in bringing understanding and compassion."

Our struggles merely expose our sabotaging habits, adverse conditioning, and unhealed childhood wounds. When we suffer, our wounded inner child[4] is suffering. Pausing and attending to our inner wounded child is how we can use these pains for our

---

4   In analytical psychology, the inner child is the childlike, semi-indepen-dent sub-personality of a person that includes what a person learned and experienced as a child.

healing and growth, no matter how unjustified and cruel they may seem on the surface.

Our defeats, triggers, and pains are not problems to be solved but opportunities and portals for our growth. We must not resent them or resist them. Instead, we should welcome them and get curious about their messages. They are the heralds and catalysts for our evolution. Rumi said, "Where there is ruin, there is hope for a treasure."[5]

> *"Every adversity, every failure, every heartache carries with it the seed of an equal or greater benefit."*
> *—Napoleon Hill*

Oops, I Demolished My Remote Control

The Art of Living in Joy is taking back our control. Imagine you are a rental agency or a real estate investor. Do you ever pay someone to rent a house from you? The process is obviously the other way around. People pay to rent a place. Then why do we allow people, events, and circumstances to rent a space in our head for free? It seems we're even paying them by overthinking, overgeneralizing, fortune-telling, catastrophizing, and excessive self-criticism.

If we think about it, giving power to anyone or anything to make us sad or happy is absurd. Which one of these sounds familiar? I will be happy when I pass the exam, graduate, find that job, get married, buy that car, purchase that house, have a child, have a second child, move to another city, go on that vacation, earn more money, have more clients, get that promotion, climb the corporate ladder, or conquer this grave disease. When we look outside to soothe our pain, we are at the mercy of an external agent, which we have zero control over.

Feeling joyful is a skill. If we do not have the skill, we will never be able to feel joy even if all our dreams come true and all our "problems" are solved.

---

5   Step three of P.A.U.S.E. will extensively attend to understanding and deciphering thoughts and triggers

Joy does not need a reason. It is a state of mind and can be cultivated anywhere and anytime, whether in sickness or health, with money or without, alone or in a relationship. We live in a mental world. There is nothing outside of us. Even the objects in the outside world are perceived within us when their images are formed on our retinas.

When a friend, a client, or a colleague doesn't respond to our text, email, or phone call, either we can feel horrible by fabricating a story in our head, or we can assume they broke their phone or are preoccupied with an urgent situation.

Almost always, even in the most challenging situations, we can override our primitive brain's mechanism that unconsciously comes up with the worst possible scenario and instead choose an empowering story to appease our nerves. The choice is ours. The only sane thing to do is to eradicate our remote control so that nothing on the outside gets a chance to turn our happiness on or off.

You are Enough, Worthy, and Whole

Once we know our happiness is inherent and independent of outside stimuli, we are free. Once we believe we are enough, whole, and worthy in our essence, we are liberated. Once we understand that the tenacious need to be more, do more, and have more is merely a program that was installed in us by our caregivers, we can step out of Plato's cave and abandon our shackles of not-enoughness.

Rumi said, "This place is a dream. Only a sleeper considers it real. Then death comes like dawn, and you wake up laughing at what you thought was your grief."

As one of my teachers advised, every morning in my meditation ritual I declare, "I destroy my life." This not only helps me embody the impermanence of earthly life, it empowers me for a moment to live my pure essence empty of my belongings. This is the zone of unadulterated consciousness and cosmic awareness.

At least for a moment in my day, I am not a mother, a wife, a daughter, a friend, a business owner, a coach, or a woman. I do not have a role, a label, a name, or even a body. I own nothing and I am not afraid of losing anything. I am solely the witness of existence, the admirer of creation, and the receiver of cosmic love. I am empty of all judgments, expectations, and conditioning.

It's imperative to psychologically understand why we feel we are not enough, why we almost always look for approval from others, and why we subconsciously feel unseen, unheard, unworthy, and incomplete regardless of the amount of outer achievements and inner work we have done over the years. The conditioning and the brain wiring of such tendencies were mainly developed in our childhood years, specifically from zero to seven.

If we were lucky and our basic needs such as food, shelter, and emotional connection were met from the time we were born to the time we became mobile, we had a good start. However, after we began to do things somewhat autonomously, regardless of how tender our caregivers attempted to be, we still had to follow a myriad of rules in order to be a functional human being.

As children, despite our impulse to keep playing, we were expected to leave the playground or get ready for sleep. We were pressured to get buckled up in a stroller or a car seat, although it felt too confining. We had to eat the food we were served and probably finish it too. We were expected to share our toys, when to a small human toys are an extension of one's body. We had to leave the comfort of our bed and get ready for school, keep quiet in classrooms, and talk only when spoken to. We were bombarded by loads of tasks to gradually learn how to be a conforming human.

Although these seem inevitable and trivial, to an underdeveloped brain they feel overwhelming, unfair, and intimidating. Unless our parents were radically conscious and compassionate educators, we were majorly coerced—punished or rewarded— to brush our teeth, wash our hands, eat our veggies, take baths, wear specific clothes, clean up our toys, share our toys, and do our homework even if we didn't feel like doing them.

If these were not enough, we were continually shut down or punished if we didn't comply with what was asked of us. If we were penalized and told that "boys don't cry" or that "girls need to be good," our ego defense mechanism gradually had to learn to suppress our legitimate feelings. This gave us the notion that we were bad if we became mad or sad.

Little by little, our caregivers unconsciously did their best to teach us to suppress our healthy human feelings, sensations, and inner knowing, leading us to either need a good amount of therapy or resort to numbing our pain by addictive behavior in the future.

As peculiar and dramatic as it sounds, almost all of us have been traumatized as children, even if we did not have clinically abusive parents. In our little, defenseless, barely developed brains, we thought we didn't deserve not only to be loved, but to live. After all, our existence was contingent on our caregivers' attention and mercy. Every one of our encounters with them gave us an impression that either we live or we die.

To make this even more dramatic, this is the brain wiring we have been tagging along to adulthood. This is the familiar zone of not being good enough, not approved, and not seen and accepted for our authentic feelings. This is the story of our fallacious unworthiness and how by reclaiming self-love and self-approval, we pave the path of awakening to our limitless essence.

Choose Your Hard

I uploaded a meme on social media one day that said, "Our superpower is the power of choice. Choose compassion. Choose love."

People repeatedly left comments that they wished it were that easy. Some believed that the statement was merely a naïve and unrealistic ideal and wondered how they could possibly accomplish this when people hurt them or are downright nasty. I empathized with the commenters but also responded, "Life's hard anyways; we just need to choose our hard."

Consciously choosing to rise above our ego, trying to see other perspectives, and cultivating compassion is hard, but relinquishing power to our automatic defense mechanism and eternally fighting to be right is also hard. Let's choose our hard!

Attempting to communicate with empathy and no criticism is hard, but experiencing stonewalling or heated squabbles is also hard. Let's choose our hard!

Preventing oneself from criticizing or coercing our children or partners is hard, but deepening disconnection and living with resentment and power struggles is also hard. Let's choose our hard!

Pausing and asking ourselves if what we're about to eat will nourish our body is hard, but living with obesity, fatigue, mood swings, and most other physical and emotional discomfort is also hard. Let's choose our hard!

Waking up early in the morning to meditate is hard, but living with stress, easily giving in to our impulsive reactions, and feeling severed from our authentic Self is also hard. Let's choose our hard!

Putting on our sneakers and leaving the comfort of our house to go out walking in the cold is hard, but living with hormone imbalance and low energy is also hard. Let's choose our hard!

Being self-disciplined to read for that test or get that certificate is hard, but continually feeling unaccomplished and unmotivated is also hard. Let's choose our hard!

Reserving some time for self-care and connection time for each member of our family is hard, but feeling disconnected from oneself and others is also hard. Let's choose our hard!

Remembering to use our tools to cultivate joy, love, and peace on a moment-by-moment basis is hard, but living with depression, resentment, and hostility is also hard. Let's choose our hard!

Taking responsibility for all we experience in life and refraining from blaming, shaming, nagging, and judging is hard, but constantly feeling like a victim is also hard. Let's choose our hard!

When an adversity happens in our life, we can choose to be either wounded and resentful or wiser and more compassionate. The choice is always ours. In his book, Man's Search for Meaning, Viktor E. Frankl narrated his experiences as a prisoner in Nazi concentration camps during World War II and said, "You can take away my wife, you can take away my children, you can strip me of my clothes and my freedom, but there is one thing no person can ever take away from me – and that is my freedom to choose how I will *react* to what happens to me!"

The more awareness we have and the more we can transcend the façade of people's behavior and events, the more choices we have. We start by choosing our mindset and our reaction, then gradually, effortlessly, and miraculously we're able to choose our outer world as well. Better yet, as we take care of our inner world, our outer world takes care of itself. This is because the vibration we put out in the world will eventually attract similar events, people, and circumstances.[6]

It's Really All About Feeling Good

The title of this section isn't about suppressing all the "bad" feelings. We can feel grief, anger, envy, fear, and all the other emotions, and still not suffer. As Haruki Murakami, the bestselling Japanese writer, said, "Pain is inevitable. Suffering is optional."[7]

Willingly paying attention and honoring our healthy human feelings for a specific period differs from allowing our ongoing and nagging thoughts to consume us and deplete our life force indefinitely without our consent.

If we look closer, we can recognize that we're more in our head than in our body. We barely feel our feelings, and we're primarily flooded with our unconscious fear-thinking. This includes the

---

6   Read more about vibration in the second step of P.A.U.S.E.
7   Read more about emotional literacy in the second step of P.A.U.S.E.

entire spectrum of feelings, including the "good" ones. There are very few scenarios that succeed in bringing us to our present-moment experience and make us feel joy and awe in the moment.

An example of this could be watching a sunrise or a sunset. Even then we lose awareness after a few short moments and plunge back into the pool of exhausting thoughts.

Even if we're eating the most exotic and scrumptious food, we may only taste the first or the second bite if we're lucky. This is because our thoughts hinder us from feeling, sensing, and paying attention to our present-moment experiences due to a phenomenon called mind-wandering.[8]

Our ego defense mechanism, which was formed in childhood, has been developed to mainly focus on things that go "wrong" in the moment in order to protect us and keep us informed. This causes most of our mind-wandering to be negative and adverse. Since this is an automatic and unconscious behavior, it's vital that we intentionally transform this psychological predisposition and consciously bring our attention to the things that go "right."

The best strategy to accomplish this is by cultivating gratitude. Shifting our attention to what we already have and what already goes "right" frees up our life source, brings us to alignment with our boundless essence, and connects us to the field of infinite possibilities.

One of the best tools to make sure we have practiced gratitude at least once a day is to include a gratitude exercise in our morning meditation. Every morning during my meditation, I make sure I cultivate gratitude for the blessings I might otherwise take for granted. I feel grateful for the land of the free I dwell in, for the city and the house I live in, for the education I have acquired, for my family, for our health, and most importantly, for my awakening by imagining if I didn't have these blessings in the current moment.

---

8   Read more about mindfulness and mind in the first step of P.A.U.S.E.

Gratitude Exercise

- Please hold a smile throughout this exercise.
- From zero to 10 (10 being the highest level), rate yourself how joyful, grateful, and peaceful you are at the moment.
- Put both hands on your spiritual heart in the middle of your chest.
- Take three deep breaths to your heart by breathing through your nose and breathing out through your mouth.
- Say, "*I feel grateful for___ .*" Fill in the blank at least three times.
- Every time, spend several moments to truly cultivate gratitude for what you mentioned.
- When you have reviewed all the items, keep this state of appreciation and joy for at least one minute.
- Think of a word or mantra or a phrase that describes this state.
- Rate yourself again.
- Repeat the affirmation while leveling up the feeling until you reach 10.
- Start and end your day with this exercise and set three reminders on your phone to do it throughout the day as well.
- By doing this practice for at least a couple of weeks, you start to successfully program your mind and body for this state through associating your smile, your hand gesture, and your phrase with the feelings of joyfulness, gratefulness, and harmony. After a period of brain programming, by merely putting your hands on your heart or saying the phrase, you can instantly experience the same elated feelings without needing to do the exercise for one minute.

The more we cultivate gratitude through this practice during the day, the more effectively we reprogram our automatic fear-based brain for peace and joy. If nothing changes, nothing changes.

Because we manifest what we feel, this practice is pivotal for our healing and freedom. If we feel abundant, we manifest abundance.

Abundance is a feeling that feels like joy. If we feel love, we attract more love because we resonate with that vibration. Adversely, when we feel exhausted, frustrated, irritated, or overwhelmed, there is a great chance that our children, partners, parents, colleagues, or friends match up with our feelings by being argumentative, resentful, uncooperative, or defiant.

"Your life is a mirror," said Robin Sharma. "Life gives us not what we want. Life gives us who we are."

A more concrete biological example of this phenomenon is mirror neurons. An example of a mirror neuron is when we cry as we see an actor crying in a movie or start yawning when someone yawns. A mirror neuron mirrors the behavior of others and fires in a similar fashion when a species observes an action performed by another as if the observer is acting the action itself.

To understand the vibrational attraction through an example in physics, we can do an experiment with a tuning fork and a guitar string. When we strike a tuning fork and place it on a guitar, only the specific string tuned to the same frequency as the tuning fork will vibrate and all other strings remain unaffected. Similarly, our outer world vibrates according to our inner frequency.

This is why it's pivotal that we always start from within. How much of the outside world can we control anyways? Probably little to none. Although it's also challenging to take control of our inner state, it's still more possible to make an inner change than an outer one.

I got to fully understand this phenomenon after the scamming incident. Although the lesson it gifted me didn't come for free, nothing could have so magnificently inspired me to embody this principle. I attracted lack because I was vibrating on lack already.

Developing and teaching the Art of Living in Joy for many years was one thing, but being adamant to pause as much as I could to not get sucked into the doing part of life and be grateful and joyful on a moment-by-moment basis was another.

I could not have come this far without the irritant in my shell. The pearl is in feeling good. We might be able to access the state of feeling good momentarily throughout the day, but it's crucial to continually try to expand these states as well as increase their frequency as much as we can.

That is why having daily personal healing routines is paramount. If we want to attract more clients, we must first feel good. If we want to see more zeros at the end of our bank balance, we must first feel good. If we want to manifest a healthier body, we must first feel good. If we want to attract the "perfect" partner, we must first feel good. If we want our children to cooperate and clean their room with a good attitude, we must first feel good. If we want to get that promotion, we must first feel good. If we want to ask someone for a favor, we must first feel good. Even if we do not achieve what our heart desires, we have lost nothing. At least we felt good!

Joy is Happiness Without a Reason

When the only horse of a farmer escaped, his neighbors sympathized with him on his "bad" luck. In response to their commiserating, he answered, "Good luck? Bad luck? Who knows?"

A couple of days later, the horse returned accompanied with a herd of wild horses. This time the neighbors congratulated him on his "good" luck. Repeating what he previously said, he replied, "Good luck? Bad luck? Who knows?"

Several days later, his son broke his leg when he attempted riding one of the wild horses. Once again, everyone shared their comments of how unlucky he was when he responded once again, "Good luck? Bad luck? Who knows?"

The next day government delegates came to recruit his son for a bloody war and the son was dismissed because of his broken leg. Now do you think this was good luck or bad luck? Who knows?

Joy is unconditional happiness. It's a state of mind that we can cultivate regardless of any inside or outside stimuli. Even our less-than-optimal bodily condition, along with our physical and emotional pain, can be deemed irrelevant to our states of equanimity and joyous presence. Pain exists in our body, but suffering resides in our thoughts and our interpretations. It's possible to feel grief, envy, fear, anger, and all other difficult feelings and not suffer.

While happiness is transient and is usually associated with achieving a goal, joy can be accessed at a moment's notice without an excuse because it's our inherent state that has been tarnished by our adverse childhood experiences. The more we practice living in this state, the more frequently we can access it.

Since childhood, we have been injected with the idea that we need to achieve something on the outside in order to feel worthy inside. Instead of learning to celebrate the present moment, we were coerced to achieve more in the future. When we entered the world as an adult, societal conditioning reinforced this dynamic. We were consciously or unconsciously pressured to have more, do more, and be more.

We started by achieving good grades in school, excelling in sports, going to college and acquiring distinguished degrees, getting a good-paying job, and climbing the corporate ladder. Then we were mass-mesmerized to purchase a car, a house, and maybe a boat, get married and have at least two children and a pet, and then take an annual vacation to temporarily get out of the rat race. Finally, we subliminally got the urge to share our happy moments on social media with the hopes of persuading ourselves we lead a fulfilled life.

The pattern of "have, do, be" was instilled in us over and over, not only through our childhood experiences but by a phenomenon called social conformity. We were told that we needed to have something first, so we could do what we thought was necessary and then be happy because of it.

For example, we needed to have a university degree so we could find a good job and finally be happy.

Like a fish that keeps asking where the water is, how could we recognize that this was a flawed plan and that the correct way to go about this is actually *"be, do, have"*? If we are intentional to first *be* grateful, peaceful, and joyful for all that we are blessed with in the moment, we can effortlessly and wondrously get inspired to *do* what is aligned with our goals and desires, finally achieving what we aspire to *have*. The secret is in the present moment and all it contains.

This is best described by a story Dr. Joe Vitale, a prolific author, told when he was able to transform from being homeless, broke, and alone to a famed millionaire. At a turning point in his life, he decided to be grateful for a pencil he was holding because he could either write a suicide note with it or a best-selling book. As soon as he was able to cultivate gratitude for the pencil, he was empowered to choose the second option. Since then he has published tens of books and is best known for his role in the well-known movie *The Secret,* which emphasized the power of thought on one's life.

We don't need anything or anyone to bring us happiness. The only problem is that we *believe* that we do. A belief is just a regurgitated thought. All thoughts originated because of an experience in the past. Therefore this is all a relationship that can be reframed and transformed. We just need to be aware of its dynamics and willing to eradicate our sabotaging habits as we instill new ones.

Awareness is freedom from habits, the opposite of dependency and repetition. Any "should or shouldn't" we impose on ourselves takes us one step further away from joy. We can do this because these are merely thoughts. They are just firing neurons in our brain.

A thought formation involves propagating electrical signals to thousands of neurons. This is what we keep ourselves imprisoned to—a bunch of neurons. The new science of neuroplasticity shows that we can literally change the neural networks in our brain by reorganizing, remapping, growing, eliminating, and making new connections.

We can change the way we think, feel, and act if we are open to it. Change is a choice. When something happens to us, it's so easy to believe all the stories our old brain network tells us. It's crucial to know that we are simply opening the file cabinets in our brain and reiterating what we remember from the past.

There is no guarantee that what we believe is even true. Most of the time our fear-based thoughts are false stories and a heap of lies we have been told. We later decided to keep telling ourselves these lies since they seemed familiar.

One of the most transformational ways to detach from these thoughts is mindfulness. By anchoring our attention in the present, we refrain from allowing our incessant thoughts to dictate our feelings.

If we eat, we must just eat and devote our senses to the sight, smell, taste, and texture of the food. Since the capacity of our working memory is limited, we won't be able to be consumed by our thoughts if we are using working memory's resources to truly experience the food. We can adopt a similar behavior in all that we do throughout the day.

Meditation is another powerful tool that allows us to experience the state of peace and joy on a regular basis. Since the source of suffering is mainly within our thoughts, mindfully dismantling thoughts and not believing their sabotaging and deceptive storylines liberates us from their shackles.

Practicing meditation helps us cultivate awareness of our incessant thoughts, which subsequently lets us neutralize them, transform them, or choose the ones that are empowering and positive. Joy and freedom reside in between the thoughts. Our thoughts are usually the source of our suffering.

We mistakenly assume that we possess our thoughts and stories, but the truth is that our thoughts and stories possess us. We identify with our thoughts, attach to them, and glorify them as truths. It is time now to have a do-over. True liberation is in the extinction of beliefs, especially the ones that are limiting.[9]

---

9   Read more about mindfulness in the first step of P.A.U.S.E.

You Aren't Responsible to Make Anyone Happy

Thinking we are responsible to make people happy is an example of a belief that's a myth. As a matter of fact, one of the primary reasons we get frustrated is when we want to make people happy, but we can't. The truth is that we are not responsible to make anyone happy, even our children.

Of course, we attend right away to newborns until they are at least 14 months old. This will help them build trust in the world and believe that the world is safe. However, after this period, we must refrain from rushing to make things right, right away, unless it's a safety issue.

We learned to suppress our big feelings since our crying and negative temperament were too painful for our caregivers to handle. If we are not conscious, we will inevitably perpetuate this generational pattern for our children and other loved ones. Instead of creating a space for people's authentic feelings to emerge and dissolve, we feel indebted to always make things right because we wrongfully and unconsciously believe people's dissatisfaction is a reflection of our insufficiency and unworthiness. We feel uncomfortable when we encounter people's discomfort, the same way our parents did when we expressed our pain.

If we are not responsible for anyone's happiness and no one is responsible for ours, our sole obligation is naturally to ourselves. Mother Teresa, Nobel Peace Prize winner, said, "If each of us would only sweep our own doorstep, the whole world would be clean." This doesn't mean that we show no empathy and refrain from offering a hand to others. It just means that we must first fill up our own tank. Similarly, we are instructed to put our oxygen mask on first before putting one on others.

This also means giving without expectation and not out of duty and people-pleasing. It's crucial to cultivate our unconditional self-worth so that helping others doesn't become a crutch to make us feel good about ourselves. It's also pivotal to serve others with sincerity and not out of egoistic obligations, otherwise we build up expectations and feel resentful. We must do our good deeds without craving to be recognized and also let go of the result. As Saadi, the Persian poet, said, "Kindness brings its own rewards."

Most of the time, wanting to satisfy others is the manifestation of a people-pleasing ego defense mechanism that was developed in childhood. Even though it takes a substantial amount of courage and ego-crushing, deconstructing our deeper incentive to make people happy is an essential part of our healing and growth.

When our children throw a tantrum, we feel incompetent as parents. Instead of creating an empathetic space for their big emotions to be processed, we try to fix, solve, and lecture and further exasperate the situation.

When our partner is unhappy, we feel inadequate, attacked, and criticized. Instead of effectively communicating our needs, we end up defending ourselves and further damage our relationship.

The root cause of many broken relationships is that we naively assume our partner is the one who needs to make us feel whole and lovable, but this grand task is no one's but ours. Who knows us and our needs better than ourselves? By focusing on ourselves and taking care of our own needs and yearnings to be seen, heard, accepted, and loved, we release people from this monumental and unrealistic task. If they could carry out such an enormous responsibility, they would do so for themselves.

When couples come to me for coaching advice, the majority of my work revolves around empowering them individually so they can begin their own awakening and personal healing and mastery. This involves exploring their own psyche, which equips them to heal their own past wounds themselves. Only then can we focus on conscious communication and team building.

Similarly, the majority of my work with parents involves deconstructing parents' psychological terrain and teaching them tools to attend to their own wounded inner child so they can interact with their children authentically, intuitively, and without projecting their fear-thinking.

Another uncomfortable and common state is the state of boredom. We dreadfully avoid this state for ourselves and our loved ones. What if I tell you this is a state to be cherished and not despised?

Being okay with being bored means we are moving from doing to being and from anxiety to contentment. Being bored paves the path for us to be comfortable with who we truly are without any stimuli from outside. If we become experts at this, our environment loses its sabotaging power over us and we remain unaffected, irrespective of adversities. We simply know how to be happy and content regardless of the circumstances.

Boredom is a gateway to silence. Silence is not empty but filled with answers, infinite potential, and a myriad of possibilities. Unless we devote some time to sit in silence every day through practices such as meditation, we deprive ourselves from accessing our true potential. If we are uncomfortable just sitting by ourselves without any outside stimulus, we might readily resort to addictive behavior such as emotional eating, shopping, binge-watching, or addictive substance consumptions every time we experience hard feelings in order to numb our pain.

The next time you get bored, allow yourself to close your eyes and simply bring your awareness to your body. Scan your body and observe any sensation that arises in the moment. Can you name your feelings and perhaps even feel them for a few seconds?

There is no difference when it comes to children. Another piece of relieving news I give parents is that they don't have to feel burdened and guilty when their children say they are bored. Boredom is not only good but essential. It's the mother of invention and creativity. It allows the kids to look for a toy that they haven't played with for a long time or discover something amazing about their environment, and perhaps even their own ability. One of Dr. Shefali's sayings that echoes in my mind is that "children are happy with a stick and a stone." Allow them to discover their own strengths, skills, and interests.

By not constantly trying to entertain our children, we create a space for them to be comfortable by themselves. What a fantastic gift we are offering them! This will prevent them from looking for something on the outside to bring appeasement to their unsettled feelings.

By doing this, we increase the chance for them to find their inner contentment and inherent peace. At the same time this will decrease their need to look for these in their bank account, their social status, their academic degrees, their job, and the model of car they possess in the future. After all, we are raising future adults, not just children.

You Cannot Expect a Cat to Bark

Expectation is simply the origin of suffering. When we resist what is present in our current moment, we create agony for ourselves. Even if a miracle happens, this moment is impossible to change. The next moment can change, but not this moment. This moment is what *is*.

This doesn't mean that we willingly embrace wrongdoings and perpetuate mistreatment. It just means we release the energy that's inadvertently wasted by resenting the present moment. Instead, we redirect it to setting healthy boundaries.

A majority of the reasons for heartbreak and broken communication is that we speak different languages. Our words get lost in translation, intention, and interpretation. When there is a conflict, we simply do not know how to converse with each other. Instead of communicating our needs, we resort to criticism that in turn results in defensiveness, shuts down all effective communication, and gives rise to arguments and the urge to "fight to be right."

We view the world with a highly exclusive and individualized lens. Accordingly, we communicate with an erroneous assumption that people's worldview is exactly like ours. This is the gravest mistake we can make as a human race.

One of the epiphanies that can help us release expectation and suffering is that our initial intent for our words barely lands on people's ears, let alone their heart. A portion of the words, spoken or written, simply do not get heard or read. Another portion of the words are misheard or misread, and a big portion is misinterpreted according to the listener's worldviews, beliefs, and past pains. This leaves us with a low percentage of what is originally meant to be articulated.

To take this a little bit further, no one knows the real truth. We simply see a version of the truth by interpreting an event according to our previous experiences, values, and deep-rooted beliefs.

To make matters worse, because of our ego defense mechanism, most of our conclusions are inevitably fear-based. We assume the worst and expect the least favorable outcome. Instead of giving the benefit of the doubt to people, we habitually fabricate scenarios that work against ourselves and others.

Most of the time, what people think about us or tell us has nothing to do with us. We constantly project our fears and desires onto people around us. The secret to peace is not to take things personally.

Everyone wants to be seen and accepted as "right." It takes a good amount of courage to understand this and meet people where they are instead of being offended. People would change if they could and if they felt the need to do so.

When we expect people to be who they aren't and to do what they can't do, it's analogous to when we expect a cat to bark or anticipate a tree to sing and dance. No one wakes up in the morning and says, "I'm going to do the wrong thing today." We all consciously and unconsciously justify our deeds at some level, even the most hardhearted criminals.

By not resisting the way people behave or how an event unfolds, we liberate our life source and create a space to examine the situation wisely and realistically. Only then are we be able to make a decision based on the reality and not out of impulsivity or false assumptions.

In the meantime, we can attend to our feelings and investigate our thoughts so we do not react emotionally. Since our feelings are our allies and our messengers, by paying attention to them we know whether we might need to change our perspective and be more fair, honor ourselves by establishing firmer boundaries, or have more self-care.

If we don't take the pause to attend to our feelings and needs and cultivate self-love, we might perpetuate an already conflicting situation by our compulsive behavior. By using the mantra "I can't expect a cat to bark," we can take advantage of our analytical mind to put a stop to our adult tantrums.

What is the point of getting revved up about someone else's actions when we know they are incapable of doing things differently? If there is someone with the power to change the dynamics, it's us and only us.

"Out beyond ideas of wrongdoing and rightdoing there is a field.
I'll meet you there."
– Rumi

Living with a P.A.U.S.E

"Yesterday I was clever, so I wanted to change the world. Today I
am wise, so I am changing myself."
– Rumi

As I traversed my introspective journey, helped others in their path, and invested heavily in various sources and teachers, I became certain that while there might not be a magic potion out there to permanently transport us to the land of joy and freedom, there definitely is a magic formula. I spent years perfecting this formula and came up with five chronological steps that have the potential to gracefully get us there regardless of the gravity of the situation. I called this system P.A.U.S.E.

I believe the human world was originally designed to be a playground for us to perpetually revel in the joy that is inherently our birthright. We are supposed to enjoy living! Yet we were not taught how to do so by our caregivers who didn't know themselves, and neither did the school system or society in general. Fortunately, there is a new wave of consciousness in the world and it's now time to claim our rights.

With this book and the P.A.U.S.E. system, I sincerely hope you will be led to tap into your own inner wisdom by cultivating awareness of your past conditioning, rewiring the limiting programs, and adopting more empowering and compassionate ways of living. Let us all flourish as a majestic lotus rising from the mud of our past karma[10].

Before we dive into the steps, please take a moment to investigate and journal what you hope to achieve as you read the rest of this book, along with what you're willing to do to make this goal possible. Reasons reap results and our intention creates our reality.

Let's create our reality. All you need is:

- A journal
- An open mind
- A willing heart

---

10   Karma: (In Hinduism and Buddhism) The sum of a person's actions in this and previous states of existence. Following as effect from cause.

Breakthrough Journal

Journal your fears regarding health, relationships, success, and personal growth:

My fear is that _____

My fear is that _____

My fear is that _____

My fear is that _____

My fear is that _____

Write your intentions. What do you hope to achieve by reading this book?

- _____

- _____

- _____

What do you commit to do in the next 30 days?

- _____

- _____

- _____

CHAPTER THREE
FIRST STEP OF P.A.U.S.E.:
PAUSE AND BREATHE

The first step of P.A.U.S.E. is to pause and breathe. Viktor E. Frankl, the renowned psychiatrist, said, "Between stimulus and response there is a space. In that space is our power to choose our response. In our response lies our growth and freedom."

Our main mission can be summarized in this statement so that we can reach our fullest potential as limitless beings. What is this space Frankl talked about? How can we create this space and access our power of choice? The first step of P.A.U.S.E. is all about creating this space.

Fight-Flight-Freeze Response

"When there is pain, the animal instinct is fight-or-flight," said Ray Dalio, the philanthropist. "Calm yourself down and reflect instead. If you think clearly about what's behind it, you will learn more about what reality is like and how to better deal with it."

American physiologist Walter Cannon coined the term fight-or-flight, or acute stress response. He recognized a series of fast-acting, unconscious, and automatic reactions that occur inside the body to help us manage threatening circumstances. As research deepened Cannon's work, psychologists and physiologists added freeze and then fawn to this defense mechanism. Dr. Shefali also added fix to the mix, which I think is brilliant.

Fight-flight-freeze-fawn-fix response is a primitive and an evolutionary physiological reaction in our body occurring in the presence of a mental or physical threat. This response, which is triggered in the oldest part of the brain, hijacks the "smart" brain to deal with the threat by:

- Facing the threat aggressively (fight)
- Running away from the threat (flight)
- Becoming immobilized in the face of a threat (freeze)
- Trying to please others to avoid conflicts (fawn)
- Trying to provide solutions to avoid conflicts (fix)

Take a moment to see which mechanism your brain primarily uses to protect you, and make an effort to follow through with the following recipe as Dr. Shefali advises in each case:

If your protective mechanism is "fight," you most probably like to be in control, and your wounded inner child feels out of control, scared, and like a failure. In this case, tell yourself, "You're loved. This is not an emergency. There's nothing to control."

If your protective mechanism is "flight," you most probably feel you're not worthy, and your wounded inner child wants to escape. In this case, tell yourself, "You're loved. This is not an emergency. You can handle it. You don't have to run away."

If your protective mechanism is "freeze," you most probably feel you're not good enough, and your wounded inner child wants to disengage from the situation. In this case, tell yourself, "You're loved and good enough. This is not an emergency. You can do this!"

If your protective mechanism is "fawn," you most probably feel you don't belong, and your wounded inner child looks for ways to please people to avoid conflicts. In this case, tell yourself, "This is not an emergency. You want them to like you. You're loved as you are."

If your protective mechanism is "fix," you most probably are a worrier and want to fix everything, and your wounded inner child doesn't feel loved. In this case, tell yourself, "You're loved.

This is not an emergency. You want to fix it all. There's nothing to fix."

In this book, I use fight-flight-freeze more often than the other variations for simplicity.

The problem is that most of these so-called "threats" detected by our brain in this day and age are not actually life-threatening. The experience of our child's refusing to go to school or our partner's neglectful behavior is nowhere near a predator attacking us in former ages.

The most rudimentary and applicable way to neutralize the fight-flight-freeze response and create the space Frankl talked about is to actually physically separate ourselves from a conflicting situation if it is safe to do.

Roman philosopher Seneca said, "The greatest remedy for anger is delay." By physically removing ourselves from the setting, we get a golden opportunity to refrain from trying to fix the situation, give solutions, justify ourselves, or criticize others without careful consideration. These all fuel the fire.

By doing this, we get a chance to use our body awareness, such as our breath to detach from fear-thinking and reexamine our perspectives. This can generate a fertile ground for dismantling our fight-flight-freeze system or ego defense mechanism and reactivating our thinking brain so we can *choose* our next action and *respond* compassionately rather than reacting defensively or aggressively.

The recipe is simple. Pause and refrain from talking, lecturing, arguing, calling, emailing, texting, trying to fix the situation, and making decisions when you are in the storm. The reason is also simple. It's because our high-functioning brain is shut down when we are in the fight-flight-freeze mode.

When we are triggered, angry, irritated, or frustrated, the amygdala, responsible for fear-processing, triggers our protective mechanism and overrides the function of our frontal lobe that oversees important cognitive skills such as emotional regulation, problem-solving, and judgment.

This primitive part of the brain has no sense of time. Therefore we feel as terrified as we originally felt in childhood by a similar event or when we were chased by a predator. The amygdala silences the thinking mind or the prefrontal cortex, which makes it hard for us to act in an adult manner. We are virtually being re-traumatized and reliving a suppressed and disturbing childhood memory.

We need to prevent the activation of the amygdala at all costs and engage our thinking brain before our automatic defense mechanism takes over. We don't have to be at the mercy of our archaic spontaneous and primitive reactions. We always have a choice. After pausing, as we see in the next step, it's crucial to understand and pay attention to our underlying wounds and feel our pain so they gradually lose their detrimental power. This will allow us to become less triggered over time.

To bring this point home, we are not capable of responding with our integrated and coherent brain when we get triggered by an event. We get coerced to react under the influence of our ego defense mechanism, which was mainly formed in our early childhood. It's crucial to understand that the person who functions impulsively isn't the adult self but the three-or-four-year-old wounded inner child. That is why we think, feel, and act like a three-year-old when we bicker with our children, our partner, or anyone else.

The ego defense mechanism was formed to handle the life-or-death situations in our childhood when our survival depended on our caregivers. Evolutionarily, this region was activated to urgently pump blood to our muscles so we could run away from saber-toothed tigers. Both were life-or-death situations, both emergencies.

Although we no longer are chased by a saber-toothed tiger, the stress response we feel when something isn't going our way is the same response we had when we dwelled in caves.

Fight   Flight   Freeze

The primitive defense part of our brain didn't evolve at the same pace as our frontal lobe because its fiery function is still sometimes needed in our era. For example, we might need it to avoid car accidents, grab our child from the street, or in a worst-case scenario physically fight a kidnapper.

Nevertheless, the project due date, our child's defiance, and losing stock money are all modern tigers that perpetually chase us, haunt us, and diminish our life for the wrong reasons. Our body doesn't know the difference between escaping a predator or rushing to get out of the house in the morning since we have the same physiological responses such as increased heart rate, blood pressure, and adrenaline production when our fight-flight-freeze system gets turned on.

In the face of a threat, some of our bodily functions automatically shut down, such as the digestive system, growth processes, and our high-functioning brain since all the bodily resources are used for the fight-flight-freeze system and our survival. No physical, mental, or energetic resources are left for empathy, growth, discernment, and perspective-shifting. That is why it's critical that we interrupt a defensive pattern as soon as we become aware of it, otherwise we are merely left with primitive brain functioning with its reactionary and destructive alternatives.

Unlike the way our body instinctively reacts, we can all agree that real life-or-death situations are extremely rare in our current lives. That is why it's crucial to learn and practice ways to override this primitive mechanism so we can rise above our ego defense mechanism.

Since our ego was formed in childhood, we relive our child self when it's activated. We need time and avid intention and attention to reactivate our higher brain or our prefrontal cortex. We need tools to create this space for ourselves at the time we are triggered. Take a moment and think and journal about what you can do to create this space. A walk around the block? Sit at your meditation cushion? Take a bath? Do some breathing?

Taking a break and creating space between ourselves and the stimulus empowers us to recognize the false fear that fuels our fury. It allows us to detach from the unconscious belief that this is a life-or-death situation or an emergency. We get a choice not to believe a sheer lie. When we take a break, since our current experiences are simply a resurrection of past memories,[11] fear loses control and we reclaim our power from what has happened to us in the past.

Here are some fight-flight-freeze pattern interrupters that can help us calm our nervous system and put out the fire of the amygdala so we don't treat our daily life struggles the same way we managed a tiger in the old days:

- Separate yourself from the situation for at least 5 to 20 minutes to allow the stress hormone to drop.
- Remember a mantra such as *this is not an emergency.*
- Count down from 5 to 1.
- Take three deep belly breaths as you put one hand on your heart and one hand on your stomach.

---

11   More on this on the third step of P.A.U.S.E.

- Do box breathing four times (inhale slowly for a count of four, hold your breath for a count of four, exhale for a count of four, hold your breath for a count of four.)
- Yawn.
- Do mindful breathing or meditate.
- Bring awareness to your five senses or body sensations.
- Rub or massage your ears.
- Put your palm on your forehead and leave it there for three minutes.
- Put your hand on your heart and tap between your pinky and ring fingers at the back of your hand and repeat, "I am safe."
- Put both hands on your heart and repeat, "I am loved. I am enough."
- Sing, chant, hum.
- Journal your thoughts and feelings.
- Take a shower while visualizing the water washing all your problems away.
- Take a stroll in nature and practice mindful watching, touching, and listening.
- Hug someone.

To make matters even more dramatic, it's appropriate to say that due to the mechanism of our brain we are on fight-flight-freeze mode most of the time. Unless we have intentionally trained our brain to overlook the false threats or have had angels as parents that instantly fulfilled our basic psychological needs, the primitive part of our brain remains just that—primitive and archeologically protective.

Our brain constantly monitors our surroundings for possible threats to keep us safe. It is said it does so five times per second, to be exact! It seems one of our brain's primary jobs is to warn us about dangers. That's why it always—always—looks for them, regardless of how safe our environment is. We should not only be vigilant about the times that specific events and people trigger or threaten us, but we must consistently do triages on our minds and the content of our thoughts on a moment-by-moment basis. For the same reason, it's extremely wise to proactively include one or more of the practices mentioned above in our daily routines to rise above our brain's protective tendencies throughout the day.

It's vital to know that being constantly in the state of fight-flight-freeze leads to unhealthy aging and disease. A shocking truth that research has revealed is that we are in stress mode at least 50 times a day. This is the state that was only supposed to be activated on rare occasions. After being chased by a tiger on a hunting excursion, cave dwellers went to their cave to relax and recuperate from the stress. As modern humans, we, on the other hand, are constantly in a state of stress from waking up the kids in the morning, stressful work situations, traffic, news, relationships, holiday stress, financial strain, ceaseless self-criticism, and fear-thinking.

The science of psychoimmunology that focuses on the connections between the mind and the immune system shows that the mind and body are inseparable. Research shows that stress, fear, and anxiety impact the body's ability to resist disease. When we are in a constant state of fight-flight-freeze, our body doesn't get a chance to heal and thrive, until finally our immune system collapses. It's mandatory that we find ways to create our own caves and intentionally cultivate more peace and harmony throughout our daily living if we want to live a long and healthy life.

Targeting the Green Zone

Dr. Dan Siegel, the renowned clinical professor of psychiatry at the UCLA, has a brilliant depiction of the fight-flight-freeze mechanism. He introduces three zones of red, blue, and green. The red zone is when we have the urge to fight. The blue zone is where we are inclined to flee from the situation. This zone can be used for *freeze* as well. Finally, the green zone is where we feel peaceful, balanced, and experience mind and heart coherence—the state of homeostasis. Our goal is to stay longer in the green zone and come back to it quicker once we are in either of the other zones.

In their book *The Yes Brain*, Dr. Siegel and Tina Payne Bryson suggest an excellent exercise to intentionally train our brain for the green zone. Doing this exercise every night programs the brain for this equanimous state that can be accessed throughout the day when needed. Using the hand positions creates an anchor for the body and mind to automatically calm us as soon as we put our hands on our heart and stomach when we feel anxious, angry, or frustrated.

Green-Zone Programming Exercise

- Right before you fall asleep in your bed at night, put one hand on your heart and one hand on your stomach.
- Pay attention to the sensation of your breathing, the rise and fall of your chest or stomach for a couple of minutes until you fall asleep.

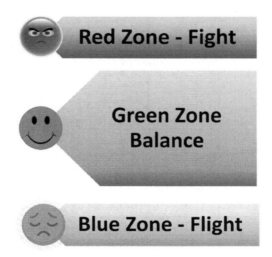

Mindfulness and Mind-Wandering

One of the most effective tools to create the space Victor Frankl spoke about to dismantle the fight-flight-freeze system is practicing mindfulness. Research shows mindfulness, with its roots in Buddhism, has gained popularity in the Western world in the past several decades due to its positive impact on relieving suffering and promoting the quality of life, physical and emotional health, and performance.

Mindfulness tools have increasingly been used by individuals in education, healthcare, and the job force. They have been repeatedly shown to decrease student test anxiety, automatic thoughts, and work-related stress, while improving individual wellbeing, productivity, employee life satisfaction, and wellness conditions.

Mindfulness is the nonjudgmental observation of the present moment both internally (such as sensations, thoughts, and emotions) and externally. It helps to create a space between the stimulus and our response. When we are mindful, we will have a choice to respond with compassionate wisdom rather than react from the fight-flight-freeze mode.

When I was writing my PhD dissertation titled *Employee One-Minute Mindful Breathing Microbreaks for Present-Moment Attention, Recovery, and Wellbeing*, I was once criticized for using the sentence, "Mindfulness is a tool to end suffering." I was advised to use "ameliorate" or a similar verb in place of "end." I reluctantly edited my sentence. However, the word "end" is actually recorded in peer-reviewed scientific research. There is no escaping it. Mindfulness truly is the path to the *Art of Living in Joy* and ending suffering.

We barely feel our feelings since we are caught up with our incessant fear-based thoughts and stories almost all the time. Joy is the hardest feeling to feel. We are barely in the present moment. We rarely taste our food and hardly live the joy of a pleasant experience more than a fraction of a second. The reason for this is mind-wandering.

Mind-wandering or "task-unrelated thoughts" involve unconsciously thinking about anything other than what we are involved with in the present moment. Although this quality allows humans to plan, reason, and learn, it comes with an emotional cost in everyday life, which causes mindfulness practitioners to believe a wandering mind is an unhappy mind. Research shows humans spend 46.9% of the time in the state of automaticity and mind-wandering, which is both the cause and the consequence of unhappiness. I personally believe the real number is way more than this.

Mind-Wandering

It's said that according to the National Science Foundation, an average person has about 12,000 to 60,000 thoughts per day. Furthermore, 95% of these thoughts are repetitive, and 80% are negative. Most of our thoughts are fear-based and lack-based because our brain is designed to constantly scan our environment for possible threats to keep us protected and safe. These unconscious thoughts are usually either regrets and adverse thoughts from the past or worries about the future.

Dr. Aaron Beck, American psychiatrist, coined the acronym ANTs for these thoughts, which stands for Automatic Negative Thoughts. Most of the time, they are not even true. After all, these are just thoughts that are merely firing neurons and electrical signals in our brain's neural networks. Although our behavioral habits, beliefs, and thoughts are solely parts of our brain, we mistakenly and rigidly identify with them to the point they become part of our identity.

If I ask you whether you believe you are your foot or your eye, what is your response? Then why do we think we are part of our brain? Why do we identify with our thoughts, beliefs, and habits so religiously? The same way we don't assume we are our limbs, we must stop believing we are the wiring in our brain.

This realization allows us to be flexible with our beliefs and opinions and practice observing them rather than defending them blindly. Dis-identifying from our thoughts helps us analyze them nonjudgmentally, release the ones that cause suffering for us and others, and keep the ones that bring us and the world joy, compassion, and freedom.

By cultivating awareness over our senses and present-moment experiences such as breathing, eating, walking, talking, and all other activities, we get an opportunity to transfer our focus and energy from our survival brain to our higher brain. Research shows that even athletes' performances increase as they learn to release the automatic negative thoughts and refocus on their athletic endeavors. The more we focus on non-threatening objects such as our breath and our five senses throughout the day, the more we can overcome our fear-based brain physiology and access our evolved brain. The moment we become aware of the chattering in our racing mind, we are no longer in the racing mind but in the higher observing brain, and this is the moment for celebration.

Since we are the thinker of our thoughts, we do have dominion to choose them. By fostering awareness, we can pick and choose which neurons to fire and which to ignore. We have the authority to think and believe the thoughts that are more empowering, positive, compassionate, and objectively realistic.

We must learn to use the mechanism of our mind-wandering to our advantage and handpick the thoughts that entail inspired planning and positive visions. Plato said, "Reality is created by the mind; we can change our reality by changing our mind."

To become conscious creators of our lives, we must cultivate discipline and practice being the observer of our thoughts, sensations, feelings, behavior, and experiences. But how can we do that? Besides aiming our undivided attention toward our current experiences and religiously using our five senses, we can fortify our higher brain by one of the elemental mindfulness practices, which is mindful breathing.

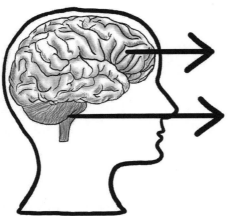

HIGHER BRAIN
Joy, Abundance,
Peace, Freedom,
Creativity, Gratitude

SURVIVAL BRAIN
Fear, Shame, Worry,
Anger, Resentment
Fight-Flight-freeze

Mindful Breathing Meditation

"You can't stop the waves, but you can learn to surf."
—*Jon Kabat-Zinn*

First Step of P.A.U.S.E.: Pause and Breathe

Mindful breathing is considered to be one of the fundamental strategies to cultivate mindfulness and conscious living. Thich Nhat Hanh said, "Feelings come and go like clouds in a windy sky. Conscious breathing is my anchor."

Practicing mindful breathing for at least ten minutes a day is a catalyst to reprogram the mind from mindlessness, automaticity, and mind-wandering to ever-increasing awareness. Furthermore, as my PhD research showed, at least three daily one-minute mindful breathing microbreaks can also have a measurable impact on individual present-moment attention, wellbeing, and recovery from stress. You can set regular reminders on your phone to pause your daily routine, preferably every hour or at least three times a day, and do mindful breathing for one minute.

As you detach from the ANTs[12] and focus on your breath during meditation, you gradually train your brain to disengage from adverse events and their mental and emotional consequences during the waking hours. This will empower you to reframe your thoughts for more positive outlooks, subsequently creating Frankl's famous space and liberating your energy for creative-thinking and compassionate solutions.

Keep in mind that your brain doesn't like to focus on a non-threatening object such as breath. That is why it keeps sweeping you away from your intention and attention.

Persevere by coming back to breath as soon as you are aware your mind is wandering.

Now let us meditate. We are not trying to gain anything, but to lose all that we are not.

Mindful Breathing Exercise

- This exercise can be done with closed or open eyes.
- Preferably, untangle your legs and arms and sit with an erect spine.
- Relax your forehead, drop your shoulders, and smile.

---

12   ANTs: Automatic Negative Thoughts

- Take three deep belly breaths. (Inhale through your nose. Inhale again. Exhale through your mouth. Breathe in deep. Breathe out long.)
- Now, breathe normally.
- Simply direct your attention to the sensation of your breathing as it enters and leaves the nostrils or the chest area.
- As soon as you become aware of a thought, feeling, image, or sensation, simply detach from it effortlessly and bring your attention to your breath.
- You can initially say to yourself, "This is just a thought."
- You can also initially visualize the thoughts as clouds and yourself as the sky. You are just observing them pass by.
- You can also visualize they are wagons on a train. Let the train pass; do not jump on it.
- Stay on the breath and be awake to this moment.

Power of Thoughts

Why is it important to be in the know of our thoughts and to take charge of them? Because *they have power.*

Change happens at the level of thoughts, whether positive or negative. The psychological reason for this is that our beliefs and thoughts lead to feelings, and feelings lead to behavior. Also, it's vital to know that these thoughts are almost always unconscious. That is why it's essential to increasingly cultivate cognizance of our thoughts throughout the day through meditative practices and mindful living.

Next time you catch yourself thinking "I'm the worst mom," "What if my friend hated my comment?" or "What will happen if my boss doesn't like my presentation tomorrow?" pause and make an attempt to neutralize the fear-based thought and preferably switch it to a more empowering one. For instance, "What's the point of worrying about something that might not even occur or ruminating about a belief that may not be true?" After all, this is our brain, not our boss's or our friend's.

Esther Hicks, inspirational speaker, and author, said, "Your thoughts change the behavior of everyone and everything who has anything to do with you. For your thoughts absolutely equal your point of attraction, and the better you feel, the more everything and everyone around you improves. In the moment that you find an improved feeling, conditions and circumstances change to match your feelings. Playing the *Which Thought Feels Better?* game will help you begin to realize the power that your own thoughts have to influence everything around you."

Similarly, Yongey Mingyur Rinpoche, Tibetan teacher and author said, "Happiness and unhappiness are not primarily created by the material world or the physical body. First and foremost, they are decisions of the mind."

Paramahansa Yogananda, the well-known Indian yogi and guru, also emphasized the power of happiness, "A strong determination to be happy will help you. Do not wait for circumstances to change. Do not make unhappiness a chronic habit. It is blessedness for yourself and others if you are happy. If you possess happiness, you possess everything."

When it comes to analyzing thoughts, it's fundamental to know that most of our thoughts are the result of *personal unconsciousness* that is germinated from our past conditioning and upbringing, specifically during the first seven years of life. Also, it comes from the *collective unconscious* that stems from generational, cultural, and societal beliefs that we have been indoctrinated to accept without questioning. The latter is called social conformity or herd mentality, which influences individuals to change their belief or behavior in order to fit in with a group.

In a social experiment, scientists found that individuals followed a group of people almost like sheep, even if the group was conducting an irrational act such as standing up from their seats upon a cue of a sound. An office's waiting room is the setting for this well-known experiment. You can watch the video, "Social Conformity - Brain Games" on YouTube. It's well worth your time.

An example of a thought formed in the personal unconscious is the limiting belief that I am not good enough, and I have to do a certain thing or be a certain way to be accepted, loved, and appreciated. An example of a collective unconscious could be that everyone needs to go to college, have a job, get married, buy a house, have at least two children and several pets, and retire by a certain age, all almost in that order. To make it even more unconscious and ludicrous, everyone believes that whoever doesn't comply with this recipe is a failure. We are all subject to social conformity unless we pause, examine the shadows on the wall of the cave, and question the seemingly nonnegotiable societal and cultural shoulds and shouldn'ts.

When we cultivate awareness over these systematically fear-based thoughts, detach from them by purposefully refocusing our attention back on our breath or our present-moment experiences, then we live *between the thoughts*.

This is the space we do our true living when we attentively see the trees we walk by, carefully taste and appreciate the food we eat, closely hear the majestic sound of the ocean waves, fully smell the rose, wholeheartedly revel in the sweet sensation of the kiss we give our loved ones, or even truly feel our pain.

This silent space is the source of our peace, our wisdom, and our bliss. This space is not empty. It's a space that, if tapped into can give us access to our higher mind before the fight-fight-freeze mechanism takes over. It's imperative to access this inner silence before our protective ego coerces us to utter those punitive words, send that hostile email, text that raging emoji, and take that regretful action.

Let's not forget all of these reactions are merely responses to our past when we felt powerless, lonely, and afraid as children. It seems as if our three-year-old inner child is feeling out-of- control when we cannot control our children and judged when our spouse criticizes us. It is as if the imaginary parents in our brain are making us feel out of control and judged all over again. When we dismantle these thoughts, we stop regurgitating the pain of the past and are open to receive aligned, well-guided, and compassion-driven words, actions, and insights in the here- and-now.

"The quieter you become, the more you are able to hear."
—Rumi

The Gatekeeper in our Brain

Besides the thousands of thoughts we unconsciously think throughout the day, we receive the equivalent of 34 gigabytes of sensory information every day. How does our brain handle so much information?

It's clear that this is an enormous amount of data, especially if it piles up on a daily basis. That's why one of our brain's reticular activating system's (RAS) jobs is to act as a gatekeeper to the influx of information we receive. RAS starts above the spinal cord and is about two inches long and the width of a pencil. It's where all our senses come in except for smell. RAS connects the subconscious part of our brain with the conscious part.

RAS is a sophisticated filter that decides which information needs our attention and what should be ignored. While our subconscious mind picks up all the sensory information, it filters out 99% of it. The interesting fact is that RAS allows us to take in information that is aligned with our worldview, deep-rooted beliefs, and intentions. If we believe life happens *for* us or *to* us, we'll perceive the world in such a way that sustains either of these beliefs.

An example of RAS in action is when we buy a new car and notice a lot more people driving the same car because the model of our car is now on the RAS's important list. If we believe this is an unfair world, that is what we keep perceiving. The opposite is also true.

Since our conscious mind is smarter, we can reprogram RAS by consciously adding or altering this list. As a matter of fact, RAS helps us achieve our goals. Knowing this, we can use RAS to our advantage by reprogramming its filter to reach our goals of living in more joy, peace, and abundance.

Let's do an exercise to understand the mechanism of RAS. Please look around and for the color red. Were you able to spot anything red? Your answer is most probably yes. Now, can you name anything that was blue? Probably not! This is the work of RAS. It brings to light what we look for according to our conscious and unconscious intentions. In this case, red was on your important list, while blue was not.

RAS is a key component of reaching our goals. For example, if we decide to be more positive, compassionate, and non-judgmental in our life, we pick up the information that's aligned with this goal, such as this book, a quote, a video, a conversation, or a course. This is why we might have had an "aha" moment about a topic even though we had heard the same advice many times before. The topic resonated with us at that specific time because it was on our RAS's important list at that moment.

By writing down our visions and aspirations, consciously focusing on what we want, and repeatedly acting towards them, we begin to notice and attract people, situations, things, and places that help us reach our dreams of freedom and unconditional joy.

Let's experiment with this. Spend five minutes writing about all the things that have gone right in your life and all your accomplishments that you can remember. Cultivate deep gratitude for them. After doing this exercise, you will notice that you will be focusing on other positive and gratitude-worthy things about yourself and your life even after the time is up.

That is because you consciously trained your gatekeeper to do so.

I give this exercise in my conscious parenting and conscious relationship classes. People are always amazed how little they focus on the positive attributes of their loved ones as well as themselves. That is why it's important to start each day with this exercise. It assists us as we continue programming our RAS's important list for positivity and gratitude.

Daily RAS Reprogramming (5 Minutes)

What is going right in my life?
What have I accomplished in my life so far?
What positive attributes do I and my loved ones have?

_____

_____

_____

_____

_____

_____

_____

_____

_____

_____

Love vs. Fear

"Where your fear is, there is your task."
—Carl Jung

Every time my daughter is unkind to my son, I notice I have two choices. On the one hand I could either fabricate a dismal, fear-based story in my head where my daughter would miserably end up being a selfish and unempathetic adult, while my son would end up with the lowest self-esteem who attracts people who bully him all his life.

On the other hand, instead of these *ANTs*, I could be more realistic and understand that my daughter isn't an egoistic narcissist. She is merely feeling hurt and out of control by the circumstances, as well as incapable of handling her emotions in a mature way.

Instead of expecting her to have empathy for my son, I could cultivate empathy for her by releasing my own tantrum and making myself available to usher her through her feelings. I could also think that my son is more resilient than what I fearfully believe. With a bit of my guidance, he would come out of this experience stronger and wiser.

Love	Fear
Present	Past/Future
Formless - Heart	Form - Brain
Essence: Connection Conscious Awareness	Ego: Disconnection Past Memories
Conscious Choice	Compulsive Reaction
Abundance, Peace, Joy, Non-Judgmental Acceptance of As-Is, Discernment	Lack, Chronic Worry, Rage, Guilt, Shame, Apathy, Judgment
Growth / Creativity	Fight-Flight-Freeze / Survival
True	False

At any time in life, we only have two states to operate from, either *fear* or *love.* When we vibrate on love, our cells are in the growth and creativity mode. However, as discussed earlier, when we are in the fear mode, our bodily resources get exclusively allocated for our survival and fight-flight-freeze responses. We have no free resources to help us heal, thrive, and find creative solutions.

Some of the attributes of the state of *love* are that we are in the present moment. It feels like joy, peace, and abundance. We are in awareness, growth, and creativity. And it's always *true* and feels *true.* There is no judgment when we are fully engrossed in smelling a flower or tasting our food. Also, there is no falsity.

Our working memory has minimal resources. This is why if we engage our brain to fully pay attention to the present moment, there will be no brain resources left to ruminate about the past and worry about the future. We feel connected in the present moment —connected to ourselves, our loved ones, and nature. This is the state of homeostasis.

On the other hand, the thought that constitutes the state of *fear* is either about the past or the future. It creates feelings of lack, chronic worry, rage, guilt, shame, apathy, and judgment. And you guessed it right—it's usually false.

It's essential to differentiate between the nagging and incessant fear-based thoughts and the occasional feeling of authentic alarms and a healthy dose of anxiety. Our internal feelings are always legitimate, and we must learn to feel them and pay attention to them as they are valid messengers and voices for change.

For example, our anxiety about a test can propel us to prepare for it. The resentment we feel when we take on physical or emotional abuse makes us determined to leave the toxic relationship. And justifiably, the collective rage caused by societal phenomena, such as sexism and racism, gave birth to positive changes in history.

Furthermore, if someone physically attacks you, please don't use your energy to send loving kindness to the mugger in the moment. Fight, run, or do anything to save your life.

As we will extensively discuss in the second step of P.A.U.S.E., it's important to honor our feelings. They are usually hints warning us change is overdue. We might need to have firmer boundaries, invest in more self-care, or simply shift our perspective. Consequently, to be entirely clear, the opposite of love is the relentless, past or future-orientated and usually unconscious fear-thinking, not the legitimate threat in the present moment.

Understanding the duo of *love versus fear* can help us be intentional about our thoughts and comprehend the magnitude of our thoughts' influences on the landscape of our life and our psyche. This will not only help us release the victim mentality and take charge of the roommate in our mind, it will empower us to pay attention to these mental activities so they can resurface and lose their disruptive power.

The goal is to question the thoughts and feel the low-vibration feelings so they transmute to higher frequencies. Then we can gracefully journey from fear to love.[13] The following exercise will bring awareness to where your mind usually operates. I can predict you will be as surprised as I was when I first did this exercise.

Thought-Monitoring Exercise

- Please use pen and paper for this exercise.
- Bring your attention to your thoughts.
- As soon as you are aware of a thought, see if you can label it.
- Are you worrying? Planning? Judging? Regretting?
- See if you can determine if it is coming from *fear* or *love*.
- Please take at least five minutes to monitor your thoughts and classify them.

---

13   More on frequencies on the second step to of P.A.U.S.E.

- When you are done, take a moment and try to remember your thoughts.
- Draw two columns of fear and love on the paper like the one on the slide. As you remember the thoughts, write them in the proper column.
- Make a note of how many thoughts you had in these five minutes.
- Keep journaling for a few minutes to deepen your self-realization.

This was an eye-opening exercise for me when I was initially learning about mindfulness and mindful living for my PhD research. I had no idea that my mind was incessantly thinking. I was also stunned that most of my thoughts were fear-based. I was supposed to be a positive life coach. What was happening?

Rumi called this fear-thinking, and everyone does it. This is why we manifest aging and disease in our bodies. We are constantly in fear mode where healing and growth are on halt unless we are asleep or in meditation.

Choose Love Over Fear

To take the royal road to transformation and create a new way of living in the world, we must choose the as-is over expectation and resentment, intentionality over automaticity, abundance over scarcity, self-compassion over shame, freedom over dependency, and responsibility over blame.

We must respond with care and not react in haste. We must choose to thrive and not just survive. And we must choose love over fear.

Most importantly, we must make these choices *over and over again.*

I want to share with you a mantra that can magically transport me to the *love* column regardless of any physical, mental, and emotional predicament I might be in. I once heard this from a spiritual guru and made it my own. Please feel free to make it your own too. It states, *"All is well at all times."*

This mantra works because it's *true*. If you don't resonate with my mantra, please take time to find your own. The best way to come up with a word, a phrase, or a mantra is during a peaceful and elated state of meditation or while you are having an awe-inspiring experience such as watching a sunset or being in nature. I will be listing some of my favorite pattern interrupter words and phrases in the next section.

By repeating the mantra in the state of joyfulness and gratefulness, you conjoin the mantra and the state together. This is how brain programming works.

You can also use a hand gesture to tie all three together. For example, you can put your hands on your heart or form your fingers in the form of a mudra while in the state.[14] The benefit of brain programming is that after a period of cultivating the elated state accompanied by your favorite mantra and hand gesture, you can instantly access the state by just saying the mantra once or using the hand gesture in the midst of the chaos of daily life.

While reading life-changing books or going on personal development retreats can be energy-boosting, unless we deliberately make a choice to move from scarcity to abundance on a moment-by-moment basis, we are treading water. We must be perpetually intentional with switching our mental and emotional states from fear to love throughout the day by using various activities and tools since our primitive brain is automatically wired for fear and worry.

Deciding to release or replace fear-thinking and sabotaging behaviors such as negative self-talk, chronic anxiety, rage, guilt, shame, judgment, resentment, unhealthy foods, too much screen time, and addictive consumptions are some of the ways that can help us in this brain reprogramming.

We can replace these limiting habits with ample amounts of hugs and kisses, quality time with our loved ones, practice of gratitude, mindful breathing and meditation, chanting, nature

---

14   Mudras are symbolic hand gestures used in meditation, yoga, and dance in Hinduism and Buddhism. They help to link body and mind and activate the flow of energy within the body.

walks, creative work, community service, and personal healing endeavors throughout the day.

It's vital to allot 30 minutes to an hour every day and attend to some of these activities to be able to readily tap into our joyful, bountiful, and graceful essence. I have provided a journal entry for you in the fifth step of P.A.U.S.E. It lists the activities that may bring you joy, love, and peace on a daily basis individually, as well as with your family members and friends.

Hugs and Kisses
Gratitude
Mindfulness
Time in Nature
Healthy Food
Physical Activity
Service
Creativity & Play
Choice

Negative Self-Talk
Chronic Worry
Rage
Guilt/Shame
Judgment
Resentment
Unhealthy Food
Screen Time
Compulsion

Love-Over-Fear Exercise

This is one of my favorite exercises as it lifts my vibration from fear to love in no time. It is an extended version of the gratitude exercise mentioned previously. I do this exercise toward the end of my morning meditation routine to start my day on a high note. Doing this practice one to three minutes every day increases wellbeing and alleviates low-vibration experiences.

It's important to put your hands on your heart at the center of your chest for this exercise. The hand position acts as an anchor. By doing this, you are subconsciously associating your high-frequency mental and emotional state with your hand position. The benefit is that every time you put your hands on your heart with the intention of cultivating the same feelings, you don't have to do the entire exercise because the state has been programmed with your hand position and will arise automatically.

- Use your mind to release all the shoulds and shouldn'ts for now. Release fear, shame, judgment, expectation, control, tension, and stress. Visualize yourself putting all of them on a tray in front of you for later. They can wait. Let them wait.

- From zero to 10 (10 being the highest level), rate yourself how joyful, grateful, and peaceful you are at the moment.

- Put both hands on your heart in the middle of your chest.

- Take a deep breath into your heart and smile.

- Inhale deep. Exhale long.

- Now mentally say, "*I am grateful for* ____ .'"" and fill in the blank.

- As things pop into your head, try to truly foster the feelings of gratitude. This is not just remembering a bullet list; it is an active cultivation of radical gratefulness.

- If it is difficult to truly feel grateful at the moment, just imagine what if you didn't have what you have at this time—a functional body, a house you live in, food in your fridge, a job that pays the bills, your family, etc. You can also remember what you might have yearned to have long before you had it, and now you take it for granted. Lastly, you can choose a past joyful moment in your life and relive it.

- Sit with the feelings as you review the blessings.

- As you are keeping your hands on your heart, check in with yourself again and rate how joyful, grateful, peaceful, abundant, and loving you feel from 0 to 10.

- Don't wait too long for the number. It should take less than 5 seconds for the number to pop up.

- Allow yourself to elevate your level of joy to 10 from whatever number you initially identified.

- Pull yourself up to the highest joy you can ever imagine. You can do this because now you know happiness and misery both start and end in the mind. You are now the master of the genie in the bottle; take charge and use it for your advantage.

- For now, this is your time to experience the joy that is inherently yours. Use your mind to claim your right.

- If I ask you to imagine squeezing a lemon on your tongue, do you not salivate? Our mind can create physiological responses in our body.

- Trust it. Use it. Our mind is constantly influencing our body and our life anyway. Let this influence be led by you and for your benefit at this time. Use your dominion. Use it or lose it.

- Do not give up until you reach 10.

- Your ego might want to keep you in fear, deluded by a story that worry equals accomplishment. You know this is a lie. Rise above your ego and declare your birthright to live in the highest form of joy. This is your moment.

- Keep this state for several seconds. You are now in the state of homeostasis where your brain and your heart are in coherence with each other. Maintain this state for at least 20 seconds. Sustain it. Make it your own.

- Think of a word, a phrase, or a mantra that rightfully describes this state. Repeat the mantra in your head and out loud several times.

- Open your eyes and practice owning this state with open eyes for a few seconds.

- Make it an intention to enter and engage with your day with this energy and see the magical power and immense benefit it has on your mind, body, and life.

- Congratulations! You have now programmed your mind and your body for an elated state.

- Access this state after your wake up and before you sleep, and as many times as you can throughout the day to continually program yourself from fear to love and from lack to abundance until it becomes accessible in the blink of an eye.

- Once programmed, you can readily tap into this coherent and joyful state by merely saying your mantra or putting your hands on your heart.

Once you have practiced the steps, you can use this short list to do the love-over-fear exercise throughout the day:

1. You can do this exercise with closed or open eyes.

2. Put your hands on your heart and smile.

3. Say your mantra.

4. Take a deep breath into your heart.

5. Rate the level of your joy/peace/love/gratitude from 0 to 10, with 10 being the highest.

6. Remember three blessings in your life and truly feel grateful for them.

7. Use your mind to level up your joy/peace/love/gratitude to 10.

8. Maintain this state for at least 20 seconds.

Gratitude is the antidote to fear and lack. If we don't pause to be grateful for this moment and all it contains and revel in the ordinariness of life, we will be forever chasing an idea of joy and happiness in the future. Brené Brown, an American research professor, and lecturer, said, "We're a nation hungry for more joy: Because we're starving from a lack of gratitude." Please use this gratitude journal to get you started on this exercise.

Gratitude Journal

Three things I am grateful for in each aspect of life:

Health:

1. _____
2. _____
3. _____

Relationships:

1. _____
2. _____
3. _____

Career and finances:

1. _____
2. _____
3. _____

Personal growth:

1. _____
2. _____
3. _____

Stop
Take a breath
Observe
Proceed with love

The acronym STOP (Stop, Take a breath, Observe, and Proceed with love) can be used as a powerful mantra in the heat of the moment to interrupt the old patterns of reacting in fear and haste. Using mantras is one of the most effective tools to interrupt old patterns. They empower us to close the file cabinets to past fears and beliefs, replacing them with novel and creative ideas based on our core values and our newly-learned knowledge.

If a train is on its way to the west at full speed, can we expect it to suddenly change directions and go east? The train needs to first come to a full stop and then change directions. As the train conductor uses the brakes to bring the train to a complete stop, we can use mantras to do the same. Saying a meaningful mantra in the midst of chaos has the potential to interrupt the flow of our thoughts and consequently our feelings and our behavior. Be vigilant since our brain gets easily habituated to one mantra. We can hack our brain by changing the mantras regularly to keep the mind engaged and interested in the process.

Here is a list of some of my favorite mantras to help you pause and cultivate acceptance in the present moment. Keep in mind that the wisest action after interrupting the fight-flight-freeze system is to separate yourself from the situation for at least five to twenty minutes if there is no real emergency. This breather time allows our mind to start traversing the five steps of P.A.U.S.E. and reclaim our right to joyful living.

Mantras to Help You Pause

- This moment is inevitable
- I am the witness
- This is not an emergency
- This is not a life-or-death matter
- Connection before correction
- Connection begets cooperation
- Control creates disconnection
- People need our love when they deserve it the least
- People do not try to give me a hard time; they have a hard time
- How can I help people—not make them—do something
- People always do their best
- People do better when they feel better
- People would if they could
- I would do exactly the same if I had the same past conditioning, belief system, and childhood trauma
- Hurt people hurt people
- Do not fight to be right
- Behavior is a symptom
- Behavior is a form of communication
- Pain is inevitable; suffering is optional
- Change is a journey, not a destination
- All is good at all times
- I want to feel good
- What do I need right now?
- What's needed now?

Please use this space to come up with some specific strategies as well as your favorite mantras to help you pause so you don't get sucked into daily dramas such as your child's tantrum, your spouse's misunderstanding, your supervisor's criticism, financial predicaments, health issues, or your emotional moods.

Having a preemptive plan empowers you to create and expand the space between yourself and the stimulus more effectively. To get you started, you can refer to the list of strategies mentioned in the first section of this chapter.

Pattern Interrupters

Strategies to help me interrupt the fight-flight-freeze system:

Personal:

1. _____

2. _____

3. _____

4. _____

Interpersonal:

1. _____

2. _____

3. _____

4. _____

My favorite mantras:

1. _____

2. _____

3. _____

4. _____

5. _____

Practicing the Mindful Pause

Developing the habit of pausing throughout the day gives us permission to choose our behavior instead of running on autopilot. For example, before eating would it not be amazing to pause and remember Hippocrates's saying, "Let food be thy medicine and medicine be thy food"? Then we can ask ourselves if what we are about to eat will nourish us or harm our body.

What if we could easily refrain from sending a foul email to our colleague that will inevitably bring us much more agony? Wouldn't it be amazing to dodge the feeling of remorse we might experience after yelling at our child over homework? Would it not be wonderful if we could pause before we talk and fulfill the wise Sufis' recommendations?

"Before you speak, let your words pass through three gates:

Is it true?

Is it necessary?

Is it kind?"

How could we do this if we don't practice? Religiously cultivating awareness over our thoughts, feelings, and sensations helps to reprogram our brain from automaticity to mindfulness and allows us to have more choices in our life.

The opportunity we are granted to have choices not only helps us in the decision-making processes or task accomplishments, it can also come in handy on a moment-by-moment basis for more joyful living. What if we could perpetually examine our mental, emotional, and energetic states and elevate them in case we are not entirely living in joy, freedom, and serenity?

The first step of P.A.U.S.E. technology is a portal to practice the art of living in joy. Naturally, fostering mindfulness throughout the day by bringing our attention to the present-moment experience such as eating, drinking, walking, driving, and breathing is fundamental to create more awareness for ourselves. Nevertheless, intentionally pausing and taking one-minute mindful breathing microbreaks on a regular basis is a phenomenal tool to be more intentional about our life.

It's time to pause and set at least three reminders on your phone for one-minute mindful breathing microbreaks. Researchers recommend linking actions with reminders to sustain a habit. Rotate the alarm labels once in a while to bring the element of newness to your brain and decrease the chance of dismissing the cue. Here are some suggestions for the alarm labels:

- Breathe in love
- I am peace
- I live with ease, grace, and joy
- Love heals
- All is well
- Self-care time
- Love over fear
- How do I feel?
- What do I need now?
- Am I at ease at this moment?
- Joy is my birthright

"Smile, Breathe and Go Slowly." —Thich Nhat Hanh

When we release our expectations and our resistance to the as-is and truly experience the present moment with all its glory, we inevitably wear a smile on our face. There is a Persian saying that goes, "Smile at the world if you want the world to smile at you." When you eat, smile. When you walk, smile. When you talk, smile. Smile with gratitude. Smile with awareness. Thich Nhat Hanh said, "The source of a true smile is an awakened mind."

Thich Nhat Hanh also said, "Sometimes your joy is the source of your smile, but sometimes your smile can be the source of your joy." While our mental states can affect the way our body reacts, researchers have demonstrated that our body can also have a direct influence on our mind. When we smile, our brain releases neuropeptides that can fight off stress and neurotransmitters like dopamine which contribute to feelings of pleasure and satisfaction, serotonin that can act like an antidepressant, and endorphins that can mildly relieve pain. Practicing and intending to wear a smile during the day can systematically affect our inner state and subsequently our outer world.

The greatest way to start this practice is in meditation. Do your morning meditation and your mindful breathing microbreaks throughout the day with a smile. After two weeks or so, you will have successfully programmed the smile with the state of peace and elatedness that can be used as an anchor later to invoke similar experience during the day. This means you will instantly feel calm and peaceful by just wearing a smile on your face. Imagine feeling grateful and serene within the snap of a finger.

During the day make it a practice to smile as soon as you can detach yourself from mind-wandering. When we anchor ourselves in the moment and smile at its splendor, we know that we are not at the mercy of what has happened in the past or what might happen in the future. We are determined to revel in the present because we know that is the *only true reality*.

"Breathing in, I calm my body and mind. Breathing out, I smile. Dwelling in the present moment I know this is the only moment."
– Thich Nhat Hanh

Stay in the Eye of the Storm

There is a saying by an unknown author, "Ships don't sink because of the water around them; ships sink because of the water that gets in them. Don't let what's happening around you get inside you and weigh you down."

By taking the first step of P.A.U.S.E. – Pause and Breathe – we get an opportunity to weather the storms of life as a skilled and mighty captain. We are then able to ensure that water doesn't get inside the ship of our mind and sink it into the dire waters of victimhood, fear, and powerlessness.

When we are caught up in the storms of life, our goal needs to go to the eye of the storm, unmoving and grounded. At these times, the essential first step is to pause and interrupt our habituated reaction as soon as we can. This helps us take back control from our unconscious ego-based defense mechanism and intentionally engage our more evolved brain to actually think.

As mentioned before, counting down from five to one, repeating our favorite mantra, and taking at least three belly breaths are some of the ways that place the fight-flight-freeze mechanism in the passenger seat. I cannot stress this enough, don't hesitate to separate yourself physically from the situation if there are no safety hazards.

I'm including two of my favorite meditative practices you can do during the day or in your morning routine. Please refer to the previous sections in this chapter to learn the mindful breathing practice as it's one of the most fundamental and essential interventions to cultivate mindfulness.

The Wheel of Awareness Exercise

Inspired by Dr. Daniel Siegel

I usually start my morning meditation with a brilliant introductory exercise to strengthen the muscle of mindfulness.

1. First spoke of the wheel of awareness: *Senses*

- *Sight:* Look around and truly see what surrounds you for several seconds. See the objects as if it's the first time you see them.

- *Sound:* Close your eyes and bring your awareness to your sense of hearing. Pay attention to all the subtle noises for a few seconds.

- *Taste:* Notice if you can taste anything in your mouth.

- *Smell:* Notice if you can smell anything.

- *Touch:* Become aware of the touchpoints on your body where it touches the chair, the ground, or your clothing.

- *Inner scan:* Lastly, feel your internal bodily sensations such as pain, itching sensations, tension, or tightness in your body or organs. Gently observe them without judging them. Send loving and healing energy to each of your organs and limbs.

2. Second spoke: *Feelings*

- Say, "I feel..." and fill in the blank. Then truly feel the feeling. Take your time. This might take some time and practice. Every time you find a feeling, allow yourself to truly feel it for at least 20 seconds. Give yourself permission to let the hard feelings bubble up. You might cry. Allow it. Every time you feel a feeling, it might transmute into another. Let it. Feel the next feeling again for at least 20 seconds. If you truly feel the core energy of your feelings and don't get entangled in the stories in your head, it might take three or four feelings to feel peaceful. Feel to heal!

3. Third spoke: *Thoughts*

- Say, "I think..." and fill in the blanks with what you think at this moment. List your thoughts, your stressors, your to-do list, and your judgments. Pay attention to them until they stop consuming you.

4. Fourth spoke: *Relationships*

- Examine your relationships with the people in your close circle. How do you feel about each one? Are you content with the quality of your connections with them or do you think they might need improvement, mending, and healing? Release judgement, expectation, and the need to control them. Send each person loving kindness from your heart to theirs.

5. Just sit in this space of awareness and radical acceptance of your internal and external experiences.

Empty-Your-Mind Exercise

Inspired by Dr. Deepak Chopra

- Say, "I am" + your first name + your last name.
- Remember the list of all your stress points and your to-dos for the day until you exhaust the list.
- Say, "I am" + your first name.
- Remember any childhood memories that pop into your head.
- Repeat, "I am".
- You can also repeat, "AHAM or AUM".[15]
- Release all mantras and sit in silence.

"Silence is the language of God, All else is poor translation."
— Rumi

One-Minute Mindful Breathing Microbreaks for Present-Moment Attention, Recovery, and Wellbeing

Despite the positive impact of practicing mindfulness on various aspects of our lives, research reveals the time commitment is a major barrier for some. I repeatedly noticed this in my own practice, where the majority of my clients either refused or were unsuccessful in committing 20 minutes to daily meditation.

As I was studying the mindfulness literature, I found that there is a need to further examine shorter versions of mindfulness practices. While some researchers have investigated briefer practices such as five-minute guided meditations, they hadn't explored the influences of brief mindful breathing as short as one minute if it's practiced regularly throughout the day.

---

15   AHAM means the ever-present and constant "I" that cannot be abandoned or avoided. Chanting this mantra calms, cleanses, and balances body and mind. AUM or OM is a sacred sound in Hinduism and Tibetan Buddhism and is generally known as the sound of the universe. By making this sound, we are acknowledging our connection to everything in the universe. The rhythmic vibration of AUM has a calming effect on the body and the nervous system.

As I was researching the recovery literature, I was inspired by the idea of cultivating mindfulness in the form of recovery breaks. Research shows that taking microbreaks such as coffee breaks, listening to music, and meditation has a positive influence on individual wellbeing, performance, and recovering from strains triggered by work demands and other stressors.

Researchers have shown that individuals who are exposed to demanding work situations experience reduced wellbeing and are likely to have health problems. They show negative effects and fatigue exponentially increases without sufficient recovery, resulting in increased stress and diminished vitality and performance. The good news is that resources can be replenished by temporarily removing work demands during a workday.

As in the case with mindfulness literature, researchers in the recovery literature had yet to investigate individual perception of wellbeing after committing to regular one-minute mindful breathing. My qualitative case study not only addressed the recommendation in the mindfulness literature to further explore brief mindfulness practices to accommodate busy individuals, but it also addressed the recommendation in the recovery literature by further investigating meditative microbreaks.

Contemplative cognition framework, effort-recovery model, and wellbeing theory[16] guided the three research questions to understand employees' experiences of present-moment attention, recovery, and wellbeing during and after taking the microbreaks for one week.

I recruited 60 individuals in the United States with no meditation experience to seasoned meditators with various professions

---

16   Grossenbacher, P. G., & Quaglia, J. T. (2017). Contemplative cognition: A more integrative framework for advancing mindfulness and meditation Research. Mindfulness, 8(6), 1580-1593. doi:10.1177/0149206315617 003 Sonnentag, S., & Fritz, C. (2007). The recovery experience questionnaire: Development and validation of a measure for assessing recuperation and unwinding from work. Journal of Occupational Health Psychology, 12, 204–221. doi:10.1037/1076-8998.12.3.204 Seligman, M. (2011). Flourish. New York: Free Press. ISBN 9781439190760

such as teachers, programmers, doctors, coaches, salespeople, managers, administrators, and accountants. Twelve one-on-one interviews, 48 end-of-week questionnaires, and 1,371 on-the-spot diary entries established the foundation to draw conclusions to answer the three proposed research questions.

One of the strongest assets of this study was *experience sampling* or asking participants to answer some questions right after taking each microbreak in the form of diary entries. Experience sampling is one of the most reliable data collection tools, as it can record participant experiences in the present moment. The goal of the study was to discover how employees experienced the influence of one-minute mindful breathing microbreaks on their attention to the present-moment experiences, recovery from work demands and other stressors, and wellbeing.

One-minute Mindful Breathing Microbreaks
Research Questions and Their Related Findings

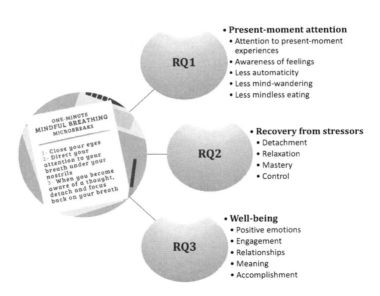

The first research question in the study asked how employees experienced the influence of one-minute mindful breathing microbreaks on their attention to present-moment experiences.

Several topics, such as catching mind-wandering during microbreaks, overall mindful living, catching autopilot and mind-wandering outside microbreaks, mindful eating, awareness of feelings, and awareness about past and future helped answer the first question.

The results related to the first question were aligned with the findings in the previous research, where it was shown focusing on the present moment was related to the reduction of negative mind-wandering and improvement of life satisfaction over time. By regularly taking mindfulness breaks, participants could better foster awareness of their feelings and sensations and make more aware choices personally and professionally. Overall, participants reported experiencing heightened attention to their present-moment experiences both at home and at work.

Here are some sample quotes:

Interview: "If I was at my office or at home, these microbreaks really just brought me back to what I was doing and took me out of autopilot."

Questionnaire: "The greatest benefit of the minibreaks is me realizing that I can incorporate presence and focused attention while doing things, not only when sitting in a quiet place."

Diary: "The thing about microbreaks is that I automatically pause and breathe whenever there is even the slightest disruption to my peace of mind."

The second research question asked how employees experienced the influence of one-minute mindful breathing microbreaks on their recovery from work demands and other stressors. Since every recovery activity can be investigated through four recovery experiences of relaxation, mental detachment, positive challenge, and feelings of being in control, these topics helped answer the second research question.

The findings related to the second research question were aligned with the results from previous research as it showed one-minute mindful breathing microbreaks were effective in reducing fatigue and increasing vitality. While individuals reported all four recovery experiences, relaxation was the most prominent experience across all data sources. Furthermore, data revealed that participants experienced heightened focus on work after taking microbreaks.

Here are some sample quotes:

Interview: "I found the microbreaks to be especially beneficial when I was getting stressed out or feeling anxious about anything. They would really help me to refocus and relax."

Questionnaire: "I was in a lot of stress at work when I started this. This helped me thrive through the stress."

Diary: "I like taking microbreaks between tasks. It's like a reset button."

The third research question asked how employees experienced the influences of one-minute mindful breathing microbreaks on their wellbeing. The five components of wellbeing according to the wellbeing theory are positive emotion, engagement, relationships, meaning, and accomplishment, which helped answer the third research question.

The results related to the third research question were also aligned with the findings in the previous research where practicing mindfulness and taking microbreaks were positively correlated with increased wellbeing. While all five components of wellbeing were experienced by participants to some degree, positive emotions were experienced to the greatest extent.

Here are some sample quotes:

Interview: "Overall I was really surprised by the benefits and how my mindset or my emotions changed during the process to the end of the process."

Questionnaire: "Well, I think it's mind-blowing. It's happy, it's relaxing, and you're just with yourself, and you're just feeling the difference... Yeah, you're just letting all the stress drain out of you, so it was a really positive experience."

Diary: "I was about to feel depressed, and this really helped me reconnect."

Besides the three research questions, a fourth theme emerged from the responses that revealed individuals were able to feasibly incorporate the microbreaks in their daily lives at home and at work. This outcome felt like a mesmerizing melody to my ears. This was exactly what I was looking for. I finally had a tangible and totally doable meditative practice that no client of mine could say no to. You can pay attention to your breath anytime, anywhere, and in any situation since you can also do this practice with open eyes.

Here are some sample quotes:

Interview: "The one minute is achievable, and I think it demonstrates that it can be done anywhere, everywhere, at any time, no matter what. I think the accessibility of this type of meditation is very practical and down-to-earth and important."

Questionnaire: "I would never have realized that a minute or two would make any difference. And I can always find a minute!"

Diary: "Once again, slept late and felt like I didn't have time for regular meditation. But I can always find a minute or two for the microbreak."

The result showed that not only the novice meditators were empowered to effortlessly dive into a meditative activity and reap the many benefits of this practice, but the microbreaks managed to amaze seasoned meditators as they were able to carry their contemplative practice into daily life.

An experienced meditator mentioned in the interview, "It was great. The fact that you had us doing one-minute meditations instead of 15 or 20 minutes or an hour really showed me that it can be done anywhere during any circumstances, eyes closed, eyes open, standing, sitting, laying. It doesn't really matter—driving, walking."

While most of my participants took one-minute mindful breathing microbreaks individually or with their family members, I recruited someone who did the practice with a group. My son's third-grade teacher was one of my recruits. I intentionally chose him to do the one-minute mindful breathing microbreak in the classroom to investigate the impact on students. Not to my surprise, he was pleasantly satisfied with the result in regard to students' behavior and attention.

Here are some more amazing testimonials:

"I have ADD where my mind wanders all the time. With attention deficit, it's hard for me to focus. Mindfulness microbreaks brought me back to focus on my writing. I don't even know how to break it down, the writing just began to flow for me. It was easier for me to concentrate. I won't say I was another person, but it was like I came back, and my mind was fresh. It was clear."

"It seems like all the stress that was there all around, it dissipates, and it goes away, and you have more clarity."

"It feels fresh, it feels new, everything feels better, you have a new focus. These microbreaks put me in that same space, in that same awareness of the attention's back, the thought process is aligning."

"It felt like a little mini-spa day for a minute."

"Microbreaks calm me, and they also let me reach solutions that I might not reach if I'm stressed."

"Every time I did it, I was grateful that I did, so it was a gift to myself each time."

"Individual microbreaks were empowering."

"Love this time with breath."

"I had a three-hour group coaching, and this felt so good to take time for me and center."

"It's so important to just take a break and do a little me-time."

"So, I do it because I look forward to taking those breaks because they help me a lot. It just takes 60 seconds out of your day to feel better for a few hours. It's worth it to me."

"I need that minute in that busy part of my day. I did feel immediate benefits."

"Eye-opening experience. More peace, less stress."

"Microbreak lift my mood each time. So soothing, self-loving."

As you can see, the result of the research were phenomenal. While I feel blessed that I was able to add to the body of knowledge by investigating a topic that is near and dear to my heart, I am deeply grateful that my proposed one-minute mindful breathing microbreaks may have the potential to contribute to increasing individual wellbeing and consequently world peace. Have you set your three reminders yet?

Notes for the First Step of P.A.U.S.E.
Pause and Breathe

My takeaways:

_____

_____

_____

_____

_____

_____

What do I commit to do **every day** to cultivate mindfulness and empower myself to take the first step of P.A.U.S.E. (E.g.: Mindful breathing meditation, using mantras,...)?

_____

_____

_____

_____

_____

_____

_____

CHAPTER FOUR
SECOND STEP OF P.A.U.S.E.: ACCEPT THE AS-IS AND FEEL THE FEELINGS

The second step of P.A.U.S.E. is accepting the as-is of our current experiences and feeling our feelings. William James, the father of American psychology, said, "Acceptance of what has happened is the first step to overcoming the consequences of any misfortune."

In this chapter, we first learn to accept the as-is of the situation. This frees up our mental, emotional, and physical resources that would have otherwise been exhausted by resentment and pointless expectations. We then redirect this energy to tame our ego and find a conscious and compassionate solution for the predicament at hand. Secondly, we learn to feel and deconstruct our feelings in the moment, so we don't become slaves to our unconscious emotions.

Radical Acceptance

"What do you mean? Should I accept that my partner abuses me emotionally, my daughter curses at her brother all day long, or my supervisor overwhelms me with unfair amounts of daily tasks?" I probably get the most resistance from clients when I introduce the concept of acceptance. I agree that this is a confusing notion at first glance. But in this context, acceptance doesn't mean non-action, agreeing, or condoning; it only means we refuse to torture ourselves with the fantasy and the need for things to be different than what they truly are. It doesn't mean passivity and non-action. As a matter of fact, it means taking action but in an informed and inspired way.

This moment is inevitable, and nothing and no one in this world can change this. We might be able to change the next moment, but not this one. Accepting the present-moment prevents our thinking brain from shutting down and dismantles our fight-flight-freeze system so we can assess the situation with clarity and choose a course of action that is aligned with our values.

Acceptance keeps us in control as it creates a space for us to understand the reality of the situation without an emotional charge. We can investigate other perspectives, examine the consequences of our actions, and finally cultivate compassion for ourselves and the parties involved. This space allows us to ask ourselves questions such as:

- Will I not deplete my life source and disempower my immune system further if I feel resentment towards my health condition?

- How can I expect my partner to be gentle and kind with me when I am unkind and self-critical with myself all the time?

- How should I expect my supervisor to be fair in assigning me tasks when I barely respect and honor my own boundaries and neglect self-care and self-compassion?

- What will I be teaching my kids if I yell, punish, bribe, or threaten them? Am I not teaching them that it's okay to do the same when they feel irritated with their siblings or friends? Am I teaching them problem-solving, decision-making, and democracy, or am I advocating dictatorship? When I don't attend to the underlying reasons for their behavior and penalize them for feeling overwhelmed and frustrated, am I not teaching them to sweep their feelings under the rug in the long run? Am I sure that my words and actions don't create future needs for unsafe group associations, alcoholism, prescribed or non-prescribed drug addiction, shopping addiction, binge-watching, emotional eating, and other unhealthy habits because I am not creating a safe space and teaching necessary skills for emotional processing and effective problem-solving?

Not resisting the as-is allows us to disengage from our impulsive reactions so we can act aligned with our values, the compassion of our heart, and the discernment of our rational mind. Acceptance liberates a space and energetic force to soothe our three-year-old wounded self so we can handle the situation as a wise and capable adult. Eckhart Tolle, the well-known author, said, "This inner alignment with *now* is the end of suffering."

Acceptance is the prerequisite to interrupting the old patterns and reprogramming the brain for the higher mind. Carl Jung said, "What you resist, persists." If I ask you to not think of a *pink elephant*, will you not be thinking about it? As you see, energy flows where attention goes.

I agree this is the ultimate challenge, but practice releasing expectations in the moment and see how your life unfolds magically in your favor. Become the *empty cup* and prepare to receive the *master's guidance.*

The mantras that help me foster the acceptance of the present moment are *I am not resisting,* or *this moment is inevitable,* or *I cannot expect a cat to bark.* As my son resists doing his laundry or my daughter refuses to put away her phone, I calmly look at them and remember the mantra. When I do, it feels like I have been purged of a burden. I no longer live in despair and denial of the present moment. I feel unshackled and liberated.

As time comes to a standstill and the space expands between us, I have more sovereignty and power to pick my battles. I can then tap into my inner guidance and know what to say or what to do to heal the entire dynamic. A mantra that helps in these situations as the mind calms is *what's needed now?*

For example, I might get inspired to come up with a game out of the laundry-folding or join my daughter's screen time to wean her out of her addictive behavior—both great opportunities to connect, by the way. Don't take my word for it; give it a try next time you are triggered and see how your calm Self knows exactly what to do and what to say in the hardest predicaments. Don't give into your emotional brain; accept the as-is and let the magic unfold.

Eckhart Tolle said, "Acceptance looks like a passive state, but in reality, it brings something entirely new into this world. That peace, a subtle energy vibration, is consciousness." Resisting the as-is and buying into our expectations creates suffering. When we rationally agree that this moment is inevitable, then why resist?

When an event happens such as our children slamming the door or throwing a tantrum, we unconsciously don't want them to do that. This is the main reason we get triggered—not because of their action, but because of our expectations.

While an event can be painful, the interpretation of the event is what creates suffering. Pain might be inevitable and sometimes necessary as it always has invaluable lessons, but suffering is optional. We can choose to put ourselves in misery by hating the as-is of the moment, or we can choose to surrender to the reality of what is.

On-the-Spot Radical Acceptance Exercise

- When you get triggered, try to witness your thoughts instead of thinking them.
- Notice the movie you are making in your mind.
- Notice your expectations.
- Are your expectations relevant?
- Is it reasonable to expect your spouse to put himself in your shoes and see the world from your eyes, especially when he feels criticized?
- Is it reasonable to expect your child to regulate her emotions when her brain is missing a fully developed emotional regulation hardware?
- Don't you think she would stop if she could?
- Don't you think anyone would stop if they could?

- Notice how you get worked up because you resist the as-is when your toddler throws a tantrum, your teenager slams the door, your spouse gets into an argument with you, or your mom criticizes your parenting.
- Notice how you *expect a cat to bark* when you desire them to be someone they are not and do what they are not capable of doing.
- Notice how you expect their brains to be neurologically wired differently.
- Notice how every trigger point you recognize in others might actually be a mirror to an attribute within you that you unconsciously resent and resist.

When you *accept* your child is having a meltdown in the grocery store, your husband misunderstood you, or your boss is being unfair, you shut the file cabinets in your brain where all memories, stories, expectations, false belief systems, and fears reside. These past files include fear of judgment, perfectionist tendencies, the need to be accepted, and so on.

Releasing these beliefs, thoughts, fears, and urges creates a space, so we can look at the moment with a fresh set of eyes and new energy. This empties our cup and creates a condition in our brain to be open to receive novel ideas. For example, if your child has a tantrum in the store, you can have this internal conversation to diffuse some of the flame:

"This is interesting. Let me see if I can visualize expanding the space between us and the entire store like in the movies. What if no one else existed here but my daughter and myself? Let me see if I can allow her to move through her big emotions without me wanting her to stop. Let me see if I can find out what my own feelings and thoughts are. What am I afraid of? What am I feeling? Maybe I should just feel my feelings for ten seconds and see how it goes. Do I feel ashamed? Do I feel incompetent? Do I have a fear of judgment? Let me feel them one by one. How about if I leave the grocery line, take a break, and come back later?" Do you see? These are all the inspiring and helpful thoughts that have the potential to come to life *if and only if* we create the space for them to do so. Does this not feel like escaping Ground-hog Day?

Sadhguru, a renowned Indian teacher, said, "Happiness is the acceptance of the present moment." Do you see how? Happiness by definition is felt when we have something we want. If we are not happy with what we have or who we are now, who guarantees that we will ever be happy?

Can we not cultivate happiness by refusing to battle with what we have? If we aren't in resistance to the present moment, are we not fully content with our life on a moment-by-moment basis? Is our life not made up of these moments? Does this not mean that we will be overall content with our lives and live joyfully? It seems mindfulness and radical acceptance of the as-is truly are the pathways toward ultimate graceful, easeful, and abundant living.

> *"If you are depressed, you are living in the past.*
> *If you are anxious, you are living in the future.*
> *If you are at peace, you are living in the present."*
> *—Lao Tzu*

Welcoming Emotions

Acceptance also includes accepting our emotional terrain and feeling our feelings. Alan Watts, a renowned English philosophical writer, said, "We cannot be more sensitive to pleasure without being more sensitive to pain."

Similarly, Dr. Siegel recommends parents to promote emotional literacy with children by stating, "Parents who speak with their children about their feelings have children who develop emotional intelligence and can understand their own and other people's feelings more fully."

The reason we are mainly emotionally illiterate is because our parents didn't follow through with this advice. As children, we were expert at allowing our feelings to bubble up and dissolve. It seems we were in alignment with what Shamans say, "If it comes up, it comes up to leave."

We used to cry, nag, yell, and scream when we felt the urge without censoring ourselves until our caregivers robbed us of this skill. When our difficult emotions made our caregivers uncomfortable, instead of creating a safe space for us to process our feelings, they repeatedly manipulated us to suppress them via some sort of punishment or reward. This is because they viewed our adverse feelings as a reflection of themselves. We made them unhappy by our unhappiness, so they tried their best to deter us from our authentic and healthy feelings.

Instead of coaching us through our feelings in our inner world, they tried to manipulate our behavior in the outer world. Instead of validating and empathizing with our feelings that originally gave rise to our misbehavior, they directly went to punishment or reward to "fix" the behavior. This is because they were uncomfortable with the anxiety our feelings stirred in them and saw our behavior and feelings as a reflection of their incompetence.

If we fail to feel our feelings, the sabotaging power underlying the repressed emotions coerces us to have impulsive reactions that aren't aligned with our values, like a dormant volcano that eventually erupts. Our ego defense mechanism was wired in childhood to suppress our feelings because we were barely allowed to feel and express our feelings. Our pain, our cries, and our complaints made our caregivers uncomfortable. As children, we were penalized for crying and making a fuss, for throwing tantrums and being cranky, or even for being too loud with excitement.

This not only caused our brain to create a fight-flight-freeze ego defense mechanism, but it forced us to suppress our legitimate feelings to merely survive. That is why we feel like stubborn children when we are triggered; the same wiring is being fired.

You see, it is not us in a fight; it is our wounded inner child and its ego protective mechanism. It's hard to fathom, but we all have sleeping little undeveloped children in us that wake up with a tantrum years later when we are in a fight-flight-freeze situation.

As adults, it's our responsibility to dismantle the ego defense mechanism, get to know and re-parent this child-self, and make him or her feel safe by taking charge of the situation with empathy and adult supervision.

In the first step of P.A.U.S.E., we learned to pause and interrupt our hurt inner child's interference. In this step, we begin to dig deeper and rewire our brain for adult-like behavior based on compassion and discernment rather than giving in to immature outbursts. Dealing with our feelings is without a doubt a fundamental steppingstone in the healing journey. So, let's talk about emotional literacy.

The Guest House

This being human is a guest house.
Every morning a new arrival.

A joy, a depression, a meanness,
some momentary awareness comes
as an unexpected visitor.

Welcome and entertain them all!
Even if they are a crowd of sorrows,
who violently sweep your house
empty of its furniture,
still, treat each guest honorably.
He may be clearing you out
for some new delight.

The dark thought, the shame, the malice.
meet them at the door laughing and invite them in.
Be grateful for whatever comes.
because each has been sent
as a guide from beyond.

—Rumi

Rumi urged us to welcome all feelings, not judge them or resent them, but treat them as house guests and as faithful messengers. He brilliantly said, "These pains you feel are messengers. Listen to them." As we saw earlier, Thich Nhat Hanh had a similar idea, "Feelings come and go like clouds in a windy sky." And last but not least, Jon Kabat-Zinn, an American professor emeritus of medicine and the creator of a mindfulness center in Massachusetts, similarly claimed, "You can't stop the waves, but you can learn to surf."

If we consider feelings as house guests, messengers, wagons in a train, clouds in the sky, or the waves in the ocean, they all come and go. They are all transient by nature. It's definitely futile to try to stop the waves or the clouds. Let's accept that and learn how to entertain the guests, receive the messengers' messages, watch the clouds pass by, or surf the waves.

Emotional Literacy

Let's deconstruct our emotional conditioning. This is a good time to journal.

- How did you and your main caregivers handle your feelings?
- Were you allowed to cry?
- Were you shut down and sent to the room when you had big emotions?
- Were you told, "Boys don't cry"?
- Were you told, "Talk, don't cry"?
- How did your main caregivers handle their own emotions? Did they show you their vulnerable side?

Our main caregivers did their best to manipulate us to stop feeling what we rightfully needed to feel. We were either punished or distracted and never allowed a space or permission to feel our grief, jealousy, anger, fear, and other healthy human feelings because our parents could not see beyond our behavior.

What did Rumi mean when he said, "The cure for pain is in the pain"? It definitely does not mean to ignore the feeling, suppress it, judge it, or blame yourself for having it. It's imperative that we get to know our feelings and learn how to feel them.

This is essential in a healing journey, and it's best to do it early in the day and visit it often throughout the day. When we get curious about our feelings, pay attention to them, and feel them, we observe they are usually stacked on top of each other.

The best example is anger. Anger is impregnated with loads of adverse feelings that have been accumulated over time beginning in childhood. While an enraged person may seem powerful and intimidating, acting in rage gives the person a false sense of power and helps to temporarily appease the unfelt feelings beneath the surface.

Anger is usually a secondary emotion, the tip of a ginormous iceberg of overwhelm, rejection, embarrassment, hurt, fear, disappointment, helplessness, frustration, shame, guilt, jealousy, anxiety, insecurity, and depression. That is why we should never be fooled by the façade of anger and always inquire about the underlying suppressed feelings so we can tend to them.

We must listen to anger. Like other feelings, it has a message.

Our feelings are our internal compass, and we should learn to decrypt them and trust them. Once we feel them and pay attention to them, we heal them. What is anger pinpointing for us? Are we in need of more self-care? Are we running low on fuel? Are we giving from our overflow, or is our tank empty? Do we need to have stronger boundaries? Should we work on broadening our perspective?

It's paramount to understand that pain, by itself, is not only not bad but essential sometimes. Pain is always a sign that something needs to change. It's a sacred sign that we must learn to tap into. It's entirely unwise to numb the pain instead of paying attention to it. The pain we experience by touching a hot stove is our natural bodily reflex to incentivize us to remove our hand. Do we prefer not to feel the pain and let our hand burn?

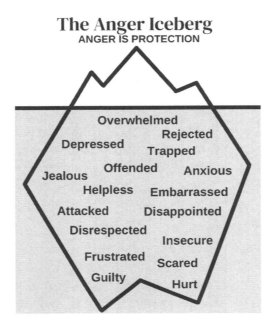

The Anger Iceberg
ANGER IS PROTECTION

Overwhelmed
Rejected
Depressed
Trapped
Jealous Offended Anxious
Helpless Embarrassed
Attacked Disappointed
Disrespected
Insecure
Frustrated Scared
Guilty Hurt

Emotional pain resurfaces in our current reality because it yearns to be attended to, dissolved, and resolved. Honoring it and tending to it allows our authentic Self to finally emerge from the cocoon of our childhood trauma and our ingrained feelings of unworthiness.

I have come up with two specific ways to approach emotional literacy:

1. The analytical route

2. The feeling route

To take any of these routes, we must initially traverse the first step of P.A.U.S.E. —pause and breathe. From the first step of P.A.U.S.E., we learned that feelings germinate from thoughts, which then result in behaviors. Hopefully, the mindful breathing practices and other mindfulness tools and concepts in the previous chapter have empowered you to be more cognizant of the roommate in your brain and you can now foster awareness of your thoughts on demand. The first step of P.A.U.S.E. is all about catching the *ANTs* and taking ownership of them.

Once we can pinpoint the original thought leading to our current feeling, we can continue with the second step because these thoughts are usually unconscious. It takes a skilled mind to be able to make them conscious and work with them. Carl Jung said, "Until you make the unconscious conscious, it will direct your life, and you will call it fate."

The Analytical Route

In the analytical approach, the goal is to first make the unconscious thought conscious and then question its validity. Because of the protective mechanism of our brain, we are inclined to select the worst possible scenario in each situation. Therefore, in this method, we try our best to scrutinize our fears and stories in our mind.

One of the best ways to do this is to bring counter examples. My feelings of powerlessness and unworthiness might be led by the thought, "I can never take my power back because of what happened in my childhood. I will always be a victim of abuse."

The counterexample of this thought can be Oprah Winfrey. She was abused as a child. Is she not one of the most inspiring, fulfilled, and powerful people on earth? By the way, was she not the first female black billionaire in the world at some point?

The Work[17] by Byron Katie, the American author and teacher, is another fantastic tool to investigate our thoughts and flip our limiting beliefs.

The protocol urges us to question our thoughts:

"Is this thought or belief true?" "Can I absolutely know it is true?" She suggests creating a space where the opposite of the verb or a different pronoun could make the sentence possibly true. Here are some examples:

Original thought: "My child *should not* throw a tantrum."

- Turnaround: "My child *should* throw a tantrum."

---

17   Check out www.thework.com for downloads

- Allow for the new thought to be true: "Yes, he should! Because he does not have the required skills and emotional literacy to handle his big emotions. His behavior is just a symptom of an unmet need that needs to be filled by me since I am the parent."
- Another turnaround: *"I should not* throw a tantrum.
  - Allow for the new thought to be true: "Yes. That could also be true! I am the one who is feeling out of control. It seems I am throwing an adult tantrum as well!"

Think of a conflicting scenario or chronic struggle in your life. Write down the thought or belief that's making your frustrated.

For example:

- My teenager should listen to me when I ask her to clean her room. She's a brat.
- My husband should pay more attention to me. He's too self-absorbed.

Now make an effort to find other possibilities for each situation and other reasons for each person's action. (Remember that our brain usually picks the worst possible scenario.) Allow space for the flipped thoughts to be true:

- Should your teenager really listen to you? Have you connected with her before asking her to clean her room (connection before correction), or have you violated her sense of autonomy or compromised her sense of competence by nagging at her over and over?
- Have you considered she might not listen to you because she feels disconnected from you or wants to reclaim her authority and dominion?
- Have you thought that a tidy room may simply not be a priority for her overwhelmed or anxious mind, not because she's a brat?
- Have you paused and thought about why her unorganized room triggers you so much?

- Have you contemplated how her untidy room might awaken your childhood wound of not being in control?
- Are you sure that you have trained her playfully with patience, compassion, and non-judgment in the past, or have you have been yelling from the kitchen every day for years?
- Don't you think we must create conditions for our children to intrinsically want to do their tasks and not out of fear or coercion?
- Have you done your part of teaching her the skill?[1]
- How are your organizational skills? Do *you* need to be more tidy or organized?
- How about *you* should listen to your *teenager*?
- What about *you* should listen to *your own needs*?

How about the belief about your husband?

- Is it possible that he's too overwhelmed and stressed about work and not self-absorbed?
- Should *you* not pay more attention to *him*?
- How about *you* should pay more attention to *yourself*?

This is a magical and eye-opening technique. I have seen it do wonders and be impeccably accurate almost 100% of the time with my clients, students, and in my own life. I am including a worksheet for you to do this exercise here. However, I recommend you get back to this one after you have completed reading the book in order to have a more broadened perspective about the underlying reason for people's behavior.[19]

---

18   Please refer to the fourth step of P.A.U.S.E. – section: competence – to learn about appropriate skill training
19   This exercise is an adaptation of Byron's work. Please visit her website if you would like to get to know her more.

Question-The-Thought Exercise

Inspired by the work of Dr. Gabor Mate and Byron Katie

Belief/thought:

- _____

- _____

What else could be true in this situation? Can you come up with scenarios that are not as negative as the story in your mind?

- _____

- _____

- _____

- _____

Flip the original thought by negating the verb and/or switching the pronoun:

- _____

- _____

- _____

Try your best to bring heart-felt justification for the flipped thoughts to be true:

- _____

- _____

- _____

The Feeling Route

The second route is the feeling path. Firstly, when dealing with feelings and emotions, it's important to know the difference between the two. Although they are often used interchangeably, they are different. Feelings are responses of an internal personal knowing, and emotions are external reactions that are made by chemicals in the body based on past conditioning or a memory. Feelings are mental experiences, and emotions are bodily reactions.

In other words, we feel the feelings and act on the emotions. An emotion is psychologically defined as an urge to move. Emotion is energy in motion. For example, we perspire, our heart rate elevates, and we might yell, punch, or throw things in rage if we don't feel and process our anger internally.

Feelings are neutral, and if we do not attend to them, our brain creates a drama called emotion. When we react in rage, we have an emotional reaction to a legitimate feeling of anger. Therefore, we need to trust the feeling but always question the emotion since emotions mask our feelings.

The interpretation of the bestselling author Neale Donald Walsch is that feelings and emotions are inspiring and truthful. Feelings of grief, anger, fear, envy, and love are all legitimate and healthy human feelings that need to be trusted. They certainly carry invaluable messages for us, otherwise we would not be feeling them.

For example, maybe it's time to set a firm boundary since we are constantly angry about a relationship or a situation. Or maybe it's time to process the grief we have avoided, otherwise we might experience depression. These feelings need to be attended and honored. If we do not feel them, they transmute into unhealthy emotions.

If we do not feel our grief, it turns into depression.
If we do not feel our anger, it turns into rage.
If we do not feel our fear, it turns into panic.
If we do not feel our envy, it turns into jealousy.
If we do not feel our love, it turns into possessiveness.

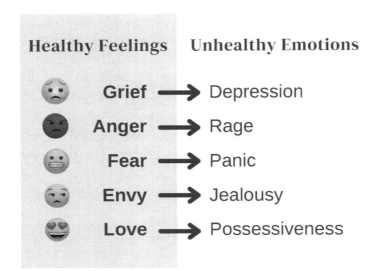

Healthy Feelings		Unhealthy Emotions
Grief	→	Depression
Anger	→	Rage
Fear	→	Panic
Envy	→	Jealousy
Love	→	Possessiveness

While the first four sets make sense, the fifth duo, love and possessiveness, is thought-provoking. My experience has shown that people who cannot feel and express their love for themselves, others, and the cosmos have the tendency to hoard and acquire things in an unbalanced manner. This could be an example of a husband who is excessively possessive toward his wife or hoarders who are shopaholics or are incapable of purging their unnecessary possessions. Overeating might be the symptom of not feeling love and admiration for ourselves and our condition.

Sometimes, it's hard to pinpoint the feeling and feel it. One of the excellent ways to prevent feelings from transmuting into unhealthy emotions is to bring awareness to the body. In this somatic method, it's important to detach from the stories in our mind and pay attention to our bodily sensations.

If you catch yourself getting angry, pause and scan your body. Do you feel tightness in your chest? Do you feel heat in your body? Are your palms sweating? Pay attention to your bodily impulses.

What does your body need to do? Do your hands need to shake? Do your feet need to stomp? Give the impulses a try. Shake your hands, rub your legs, or put your hands on your heart. Can you feel how your anger might have subsided by merely paying attention to its manifestation in your body?

Tapping or emotional freedom technique (EFT) and energy medicine movements also have somatic elements that can help us process our emotional distress and calm our nervous system. I highly recommend researching them an choosing your favorite technique.

When it comes to interpersonal relationships, our unfelt feelings are the number one cause for sabotage and failure. If we do not feel our feelings, we project our emotions onto others.

For example, if your children are not allowed or coached to feel their frustration, they might lash out at their siblings. This is the phenomenon that we call sibling rivalry. When you don't pay attention to your feeling of powerlessness in your current situation, you might get irritated when your partner, parents, or children defy you because they make you feel even more powerless.

It takes a tremendously broadened perspective and a healed heart to be able to stop assuming people are responsible for our old childhood wounds. Taking charge of our inner wounds liberates us and helps us not to be at the mercy of our loved ones.

When we feel our feelings, we dismantle the explosive behavioral reaction, which consequently creates a space for us to choose our behavior rather than reacting on a primitive fight-flight-freeze manner.

Let's review Viktor E. Frankl's saying again: "Between stimulus and response, there is a space. In that space is our power to choose our response. In our response lies our growth and our freedom." This is the space we need to create within ourselves to feel our feelings or investigate our thoughts before exhibiting any outward behavior.

Going the emotional route means we use the space to uncover our feelings and allow ourselves to feel them for several seconds. This does not involve ruminating about the story in our brain but only feeling the core energy of the feeling. This is why Rumi said, "The cure for pain is in the pain." By feeling the pain, we make a suppressed experience resurface and allow it to dissolve. This is how blocked emotions lose their sabotaging power and we are unleashed from their chains.

When you wake up, allow at least one minute to inquire into your feelings. Say, "I feel," and then fill in the blank. Name it to tame it! Feel the feeling for several seconds until it dissolves.

Research shows the duration of each feeling is a maximum of 90 seconds. You might shed a few tears, which is cathartic since crying releases oxytocin, the feel-good chemical that takes the physical and emotional pain away and makes us calm.

Inquire again and find the next feeling. Feel that one too for several seconds until it dissipates. Continue this until you access a space of peace and pure consciousness, where polarity, the good and the bad, and the happy and the sad vanish, and you merely become a witness of all things.

Remember Rumi's saying, "Out beyond the wrong-doing and the right-doing, there is a field, I'll meet you there."

This is the field we want to tap into as much as we can. Not identifying with our thoughts, together with feeling our feelings, make this possible.

You might need to feel around three or four feelings as they transmute into each other once you pay attention to them and feel them. For example, you might start with anger that morphs into helplessness, then into loneliness, and finally grief. You might also start with shame and end with peace after allowing yourself to feel the core energy of shame for several seconds.

To recap, our ego defense mechanism was developed to suppress our feelings in order to help us survive the un-consciousness of our caregivers in childhood. We were neither coached through our big emotions nor allowed to feel our pain. As our crying, whining, tantrums, and even our flamboyant enthusiasm made our parents uncomfortable, we unconsciously learned to be disconnected from our authentic feelings to avoid punishment and abandonment.

Dr. Gabor Mate, the renowned addiction expert and physician states this brilliantly. He says, to survive childhood, we had no choice but to sacrifice the need for authenticity for the more crucial need for attachment. In other words, we unconsciously thought, "If I'm authentic, my parents will reject me. If I express what I feel, my parents can't handle it, so I have to suppress my feelings." And as a result, we turn 20, 30, 40, and 50, and we don't know who we are and aren't in touch with our feelings and desires. To make matters worse, we unconsciously continue sacrificing our authenticity for attachment, feelings of belonging, and the need to be approved by anyone we come in contact with in adulthood.

As we perpetuated our inauthenticity, our inner psyche became impregnated with suppressed emotions and loads of unconscious sabotaging. When we pay attention to our feelings, they resurface and have no choice but to lose their destructive control over us. Feel your feelings, see the magical transformation, and let the healing commence. *Feel to heal!*

When we encounter a low-vibration sensation or feeling, we have two choices. We can either investigate the thought, question and then flip it, or we can pay attention to the feeling and feel it to heal it. Sometimes going through one method is enough, and other times both are needed depending on the gravity and complexity of the situation.

Please use the information in this chapter to cultivate awareness of your inner landscape and practice both approaches to befriend yourself and the suppressed pieces of your psyche. Journal your experiences for a few days until you can breeze through both methods with ease, grace, and joy. Celebrate and honor yourself every time you handle a conflict with compassion rather than letting your emotions run the show.

If you slip, don't dwell on it. Accept your humanness and get back on track. You will get plenty of opportunities to strengthen the muscle of mindfulness and pausing. Celebrate your quick turnaround and start again. This is not a race and there is no time limit for a healing journey.

As a matter of fact, the more you allow yourself to be who you are and feel what you feel, the faster the process. The more you resist your hard feelings and the more shame you feel about them, the more persistent they become. Handle yourself with elegance. You deserve love and compassion. Sit with your feelings in acceptance and let them emerge, then release them. Practice. Practice. Practice.

Hurt People Hurt People

When developing or teaching emotional literacy, it's immensely important to remember that any negative thought, emotion, or behavior is the result of a past unhealed pain. Remember, "what's not love is a cry for love" and "hurt people hurt people."

This fact by itself has the potential to help us release judgment and cultivate empathy for even criminals and narcissists, let alone our parents, spouses, children, colleagues, friends, and strangers in the grocery line. I challenge you to find a criminal that was not repeatedly traumatized as a child.

When it comes to children, our response must be nothing but benevolence and generosity. Children *need* our unconditional love and compassion when they deserve it the *least*—even in the moment when a toddler hits his brother or a teenager slams the door on us with rage. Hurting the sibling and showing defiance are signs of unmet needs and a wounded inner child. The last thing children need from us in these moments is to aggravate their hurt and deepening their pain.

Caveat: this doesn't mean all behaviors are okay. It means we are aware that the behavior is merely a symptom, and our child is not skilled or capable enough to maneuver the underlying unmet psychological needs. We talk about this in the next steps.

Use journaling and mindfulness to be aware and feel your feelings and the feelings others might experience. When it comes to children, just like you would do for yourself, create a safe space for them to feel their feelings through any of the methods we discussed before. Assure them all feelings are okay and legitimate, and that they are always unconditionally loved and accepted regardless of their feelings and behavior.

Sit with them with untainted acceptance and compassion to help them move through their feelings in a natural and healthy way.

Ditch the lecture. After the storm, in a family meeting, you can mention that while all feelings are okay, all behaviors are not okay. Then you can come up with strategies together to empower them to navigate their feelings next time. Don't forget the power of role plays in your meetings.

Difficult moments with people don't have to be problems to be solved but opportunities to enhance our emotional literacy and deepen our connection. We can heal our own past wounds and strengthen our relationships with people by loving them regardless of their feelings.

In the case of children, think of the role modeling you are exhibiting. Are you not brilliantly teaching them how to handle the predicament of the world with wisdom and compassion? If you lash out at them when they react in pain, are you not role modeling the exact same action you don't want them to take?

Accepting our children for who they truly are and not withholding our love from them because of their behavior or big emotions is a big step forward. It releases the need for therapies and addictive and numbing behavior in the future. Similarly, unconditionally accepting our own inner children and allowing them to process their big feelings is the beginning of our restorative journey.

Everything is Energy

When it comes to feelings and states of mind, our knowledge is incomplete if we are unaware of the science of quantum physics. It explains the behavior and nature of subatomic particles and quantization of energy. According to quantum science, everything is energy, even the most solid-looking objects. In the quantum realm, everything affects everything else.

The visionary inventor, engineer, and futurist Nikola Tesla said, "If you want to find the secrets of the universe, think in terms of energy, frequency, and vibration." Vibration refers to the vibrating movement of atoms and particles, and frequency is the rate at which vibrations occur.

Similarly, Physics Nobel Prize winner Niels Bohr said, "Everything we call real is made of things that cannot be regarded as real." Everything is energy and has a vibration and a frequency, even our thoughts, feelings, and actions.

The vibration of our thoughts, feelings, and behavior not only impact our inner state, they also influence people and events in our outer world. At any point in time, we have all the frequencies available to us both within us and outside of ourselves. The alchemy is in the realization that the frequency of the outside is the mirror reflection of our inner vibration. You guessed right—life is an inside-out job, not outside-in.

At all times, we have available to us both the vibration of fear and love, scarcity and abundance, judgment and compassion, and resentment and joy. The state we live in depends on which vibration we choose.

Once we think of the universe as an interconnected network of energy, we become empowered to sort out our inner psyche so we can raise our vibration for a pleasant co-creation. As Dr. Bruce Lipton, a developmental biologist, remarked, "The moment you change your perception is the moment you rewrite the chemistry of your body." Our body and our outer world hear everything our mind says, which means we must be vigilant when feeding our mind.

While all our thoughts and feelings have energetic forces, some have higher vibrations and some lower. In his book *Power vs. Force*, by using Applied Kinesiology, Dr. David Hawkins demonstrated how feelings such as shame, guilt, and anger fall into negative energy attractor fields, whereas love, peace, and joy are examples of positive attractors. The latter are life-enhancing and eventually lead to pure consciousness.

Dr. Hawkins has a scale of consciousness graph. Lower states are in the contracted and *suffering* zone. As the vibration rises, the person traverses through the *getting by* space, then the state of *flow*, and finally *pure consciousness*.

The graph identifies shame, which has a vibration of 20. Then it increases in vibration as the person feels guilt, apathy, grief, fear, desire, anger, pride, courage, neutrality, willingness, acceptance, and reason. The region between shame and reason is the territory for duality where judgment still lives on.

Mental and emotional states become higher in vibration as they are more "positive" and life-affirming. Communion with the cosmos and the unity zone lives from love with a vibration of 500 or above. Joy, peace, and enlightenment are what come after love and have a vibration of 540, 600, and 1000.

Psychological interpretation of the graph makes perfect sense. Shame, which is lower in frequency than guilt, is more life-depleting since shame questions the person's worthiness while guilt targets the action. Also, we can observe more drive and passion in an angry person than an individual who endures apathy or grief.

This graph has been an alchemic contributor to my transformation. I wonder if you also feel as mesmerized as I was when I first saw it. The least this scale can do is release us from our victim mentality and empower us to finally take the well-deserved position of the captain of our ship.

This does not mean we should always vibrate high and shame ourselves when we do not. It just means that this extraordinary awareness can empower us to take perpetual ownership of our mental and emotional states, while paying attention to the low-vibration feelings to resolve or dissolve them or transmute them into higher vibrations.

The next time you find yourself in a drama, go to the eye of the storm, unmoving and observant. Own your feelings. Take care of your own vibration. Remember, people's experiences *do not have to be yours.*

Scale of Consciousness

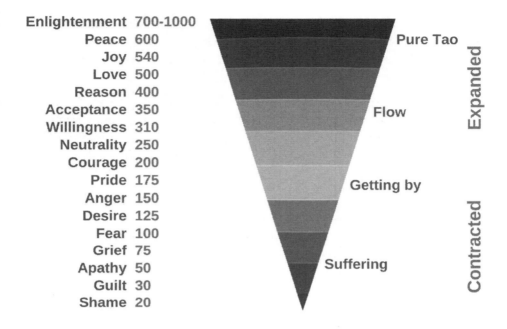

Enlightenment	700-1000	
Peace	600	Pure Tao
Joy	540	
Love	500	
Reason	400	
Acceptance	350	Flow
Willingness	310	
Neutrality	250	
Courage	200	
Pride	175	
Anger	150	Getting by
Desire	125	
Fear	100	
Grief	75	
Apathy	50	Suffering
Guilt	30	
Shame	20	

Expanded / Contracted

Law of Vibrational Attraction

When it comes to emotional literacy, understanding the law of vibrational attraction is paramount.

In the guitar experiment, we observed that only the specific string that was tuned to the same frequency as the tuning fork vibrated, and we learned that *like attracts like*. We also discovered that even our thoughts and feelings have vibrations. It seems we attract in life what we subconsciously think and feel.

If we feel peaceful, our life will be an epitome of ease and grace. If we feel unworthy, various aspects of our life such as health, finances, and relationships reflect the very thought and feeling. That is why it's essential to uncover and dismantle these unconscious thoughts and prevent them from sabotaging our life.

All this is evidence that the universe doesn't take sides. We don't live in a hostile world of punishment and reward, but a benevolent and non-judging cosmos that simply follows the laws of cause and effect. Our current vibrational attraction is the effect of our habituated frequencies, thoughts, feelings, behavior, and past conditioning.

In his book *The Hidden Messages in Water*, Dr. Masaru Emoto, a Japanese author, illustrated how human consciousness influences the molecular structure of water. He claims water could react to positive thoughts and words, and polluted water could be cleaned through prayer and positive visualization. He showed how words such as *love* and *thank you* produce beautifully symmetric water crystals, while phrases such as *I hate you* create asymmetric and ugly shapes in the water molecules. If water is affected by words, energy, and intentions, what do you think they do to us? Are we not made of 60% water?

Science of the Heart

The idea that the heart is only a pump is far from the truth. The heart is a powerful and intelligent energy center. Science has revealed that the heart has a little brain of its own with approximately 40,000 neurons similar to the neurons in the brain. It sends more information to the brain than the brain sends to the heart. The electromagnetic field generated by the heart is 100 times greater in strength than the field produced by the brain and can be detected up to several feet away from the body in all directions. It is scientifically shown that this field can affect people and even things around us.

I experimented with this after watching the movie *I AM*, directed by Tom Shadyac. The yogurt experiment done by Tom and one of the scientists at the HeartMath Institute showed how Tom's triggered feelings affected the yogurt in his vicinity. They measured the effect by a magnetometer connected to the yogurt.

After watching the movie, I decided to do the experiment myself as I mentioned previously. My daughter generally used to come home from school in a foul mood, which in turn triggered me. The vicious cycle had continued for many years. That day, when she returned from school, I attempted to cultivate a high dose of love and gratitude for her in my heart. For the sake of the experiment, I made sure not even to smile. As soon as I felt the overwhelming love in my heart, a warm smile appeared on her face.

That was the moment my entire worldview shifted, and I welcomed her home as a different person. I felt victorious as I saw the evidence with my own eyes. Her hostile face steeped in pain miraculously morphed into a face of a happy and light-hearted child. I had directly observed the power of my heart over the people around me, and I challenge you to do a similar experiment. Just make sure your feelings of love and gratitude are authentic. Energy does not lie!

Tools to Enhance Emotional Literacy

To end this chapter, I would like to review some emotional literacy tools that can help to regulate feelings and dismantle the fight-flight-freeze system on the spot. You can either do all of these tools one after another or pick some to try.

When it comes to children, remember you are modeling self-regulation every time you refuse to respond with yelling and punishing when upset. Do it to teach it!

When it comes to adults, our graceful and respectable behavior sets up a standard for our interpersonal relationships. To lash out at people without expecting similar behavior from them is simply unfair. "Do unto others as you would have them do unto you."

Before going through the list, always consider separating yourself from the situation—from 5 to 20 minutes.

- Think of the difficult and triggering situation.
- How are you feeling? Where do you feel the sensations of the feeling in your body?
- Pay attention to those parts in your body. Listen to your body. What does it need to do to release the sensation?
- Use your favorite somatic tool, such as tensing and releasing your body parts, tapping, energy medicine moves, dancing, shaking, etc.

- Name your feelings and truly feel their core energy for 90 seconds each.

- Visualize yourself expanding space between you and the stimulating event. Breathe into the space. Use some of the mantras we discussed earlier.

- Become aware of the triggering thought behind your feeling. See if you can switch the thought from fear to love. Remember, all triggering thoughts have their roots in fear. Question your fear. Is this a legitimate fear?

- Question your thought. Reverse it by switching the pronoun or flipping the verb.

- Use Ho'oponopono, which is an ancient and potent clearing technique. You simply repeat, "Thank you. I love you. Please forgive me. I'm sorry," to your wounded inner child.

- Put both hands on your heart. Breathe in safety and peace, then breathe out stress and anxiety.

- Journal for several minutes.

- Go on a nature walk.

The following Neuronal Linguistic Programming exercise is a fantastic tool for symptom management when we are rushed with heavy emotions. Once you learn this visualization technique, you can use it for a fast on-the-spot recovery tool to free yourself from a spectrum of emotions, such as overwhelm, anxiety, and rage. However, make sure you spend some time sitting with the feeling by following the previous exercise when you have time.

Subconscious Clearing Exercise

- It's better to close your eyes for this exercise.
- Scan your body for any tightness or tension.
- Pause where you feel a tension that needs attention.
- Where do you feel this sensation? In your stomach, chest, throat, head?
- Trust the first place.

- What is the first feeling that comes to mind?
- Can you name your feeling?
- Are you feeling frustrated, angry, helpless, guilty, overwhelmed?
- Tune in and name your feeling. Own it.
- Now rate your feeling from 1 to 10—10 being the worst.
- Trust the first number.
- Can you allow yourself to feel the core energy of the feeling without ruminating about the story around it for a few seconds?
- Your feeling might have subsided a little bit by now.
- Tune into the rest of the feeling and give it a shape.
- What shape does it have?
- Pick the first shape that comes to mind.
- What color is this shape?
- What's its texture?
- Now count from 1 to 5 in your mind.
- As you count, pull this shape out of your body.
- When you reach 5, see it in front of your face with your eyes closed.
- Now put the shape 1 foot away from your body.
- Put it 10 feet away.
- Put it 1 mile away.
- Put it 1000 miles away.
- Finally send it to the edge of the universe.
- Take a deep breath through your nose and out of your mouth.
- Go back to where you first found the shape and rate its intensity again.
- Has the intensity dropped a bit?
- Imagine there is a beautiful thick ray of purifying golden bright light entering your body from the top of your head and filling up the space that the shape occupied a few sec-

onds ago. Fill this space with the pure golden healing light and even expand it to your whole body. Imagine your head, your throat, your heart, and every cell of your body filled with the majesty of unconditional love and acceptance of this pure light energy.

- Feel supported, embraced, and accepted just the way you are.
- Tune in again to the space where the shape was before and rate your feeling again.
- Notice again how many you have dropped. Repeat until you reach zero.
- You will reach zero *only if* you want to.
- If you have not reached zero, know that your ego is standing in your way. Rise above it and decide to reach zero and do the exercise again.
- Open your eyes feeling rejuvenated and fresh like never before.
- The reason this technique works is that the language of the subconscious mind is symbols and stories.
- You can even alleviate physical pain with the same technique.
- Research shows even physical pain subsides when paid attention to.

Notes for the Second Step of P.A.U.S.E.

Accept the As-Is and Feel Your Feelings

My takeaways:

_____

_____

_____

_____

_____

_____

What do I commit to do **every** day to cultivate emotional literacy and empower myself to take the first second of P.A.U.S.E. (Feel my feelings, flip my thoughts,...)?

_____

_____

_____

_____

_____

_____

CHAPTER FIVE
THIRD STEP OF P.A.U.S.E.: UNDERSTAND THOUGHTS AND TRIGGERS

*If you don't heal what hurt you,
you'll bleed on people who didn't cut you."*
—Marcie Lyons

Carl Jung said, "Everything that irritates us about others can lead us to an understanding of ourselves."

One of the hardest truths to accept and digest is that if I can recognize it, *it is in me.* This is how our outer world becomes a mirror of our inner world. In this chapter, we rise to the challenge of transcending the façade of events and people's behavior for the sake of uncovering the layers of our own psyche to heal our past wounds.

This world is a mirror. If we want our children to be respectful, we must be respectful. If we want our spouse to show empathy, we must show empathy. If we want money, we must first feel abundant. If we want world peace, we must cultivate inner peace. If we want to live a joyful life, we must foster gratitude on a moment-by-moment basis regardless of the outside circumstances.

When we have an adverse experience with people or events, we are being ushered to discover our past wounds, pay attention to them, and give them an opportunity to heal. This work is not for the faint of heart.

Rumi said, "If you are irritated by every rub, how will your mirror be polished?" The good news is that if we persevere, rise above our ego, and acquire a learner-mind, we receive a phenomenal chance to bring light to our dark side and fully integrate the light that we are.

Rumi also said, "The wound is the place where the light enters you." When we spot a shadow within us, we get an opportunity to recognize what is blocking the light so we can dissolve it.

Mechanism of the Mind

To understand why we get triggered or even why we think, feel, and behave the way we do, it's essential to know the mechanism of the mind. We can talk about the mind in many ways, but one of the ways is to think of an iceberg and divide the mind into the conscious and subconscious mind.

The conscious mind is where our conscious intentions reside.

As mentioned previously, I was genuinely excited about Dr. Markham's *vow of yellibacy*. I was pumped up and had all the intention to follow through with it. And I did, but it lasted for barely a day or two. The reason was that my intention was residing in 5% of my mind, while 95% of the iceberg under the surface hindered me from keeping my vow. It was similar to a person making all the effort to row a boat, unaware that the boat is shackled by an anchor.

I had no idea of all the subconscious psychological programs that kicked in when I was triggered. My reactivity patterns were the work of underlying, deep-rooted conditioning that sabotaged me to abandon my vow in a blink of an eye. In the heat of the moment, I either completely forgot about my intention or I had no power to follow through.

The language of the conscious mind is words, and it follows linear logic. It processes information with a speed of 2,000 bits of information per second compared to the subconscious mind, which processes 400 billion bits per second. The language of the subconscious mind is symbols, stories, and feelings. This is where our past wounds, conditioned patterns, and limiting beliefs exist.

Now I have some bad news and some good news. The bad news is that there is a protection wall between the conscious mind and the subconscious mind that makes it hard to cross over.

The subconscious mind is our comfort zone. It's familiar, and it seems less dangerous because we are used to it. As soon as we choose to think, feel, or behave differently, an alarm goes off warning the ego of new and unfamiliar territory. An example is the program of *procrastination* or *fear-of-failure*. These are the subconscious programs that hinder us from taking a novel action and behaving differently in a situation.

In the case of parenting, the hindering program underneath our trigger could be the *fear of losing control* or *powerlessness*. While we have all the intention to validate our children's feelings and attend to their unmet needs, their non-compliance still triggers us since it invokes feelings of helplessness and being out-of-control.

The Mind Iceberg

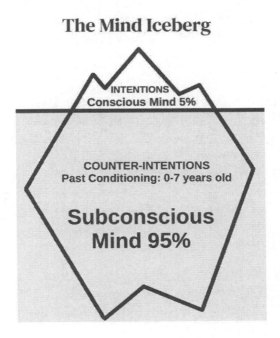

INTENTIONS
Conscious Mind 5%

COUNTER-INTENTIONS
Past Conditioning: 0-7 years old

Subconscious
Mind 95%

This is a cultural and societal program as much as it's familial. The myth says that parents need to be in control. They are the authority. The child who doesn't obey is a spoiled brat who has an incompetent parent. All these limiting beliefs and familial, cultural, and societal programs reside in the subconscious mind.

Let me give you the baby elephant conditioning story, which is a sad story on so many levels. However, it gets the point across. People who train elephants for performance in circuses or other venues start tying a rope around the elephant's leg and attaching it to a pole when the elephant is a baby. The elephant is incapable of freeing himself from the pole because he is not strong enough. As the elephant grows, however, he becomes immensely stronger than what he was as a baby, so much so that extracting the pole becomes nothing but a ridiculously doable job. But guess what? He never attempts to free himself because he has been conditioned from childhood that he isn't strong enough to do so.

In some ways we are all that baby elephant. Our programming is so powerful that our conscious intention alone can rarely make things happen. This is why we must practice rewiring our brain for more empowering patterns.

There is an underlying scientific reason behind the baby-elephant-conditioning syndrome. According to Dr. Bruce Lipton, most of the subconscious programming is established from 0 to 7 years of age. This is because of the very low-frequency brainwaves during this time. You and I are now functioning on a Beta brain wave (13-50 Hz) as we are in an ordinary waking consciousness. Children spend their time in Delta brain waves (below 4 Hz) from 0 to 2 years old, in Theta brain waves (4-8 Hz) from 2 to 6 years old, and in Alpha brain waves (8-13 Hz) between 6 and 12 years old.

As children, we practically live in the state of hypnosis until six years and even up to age 12. This makes the brain enormously suggestible during these years, similar to a sponge. This is when all our mental, emotional, and behavioral patterns get downloaded in the subconscious mind.

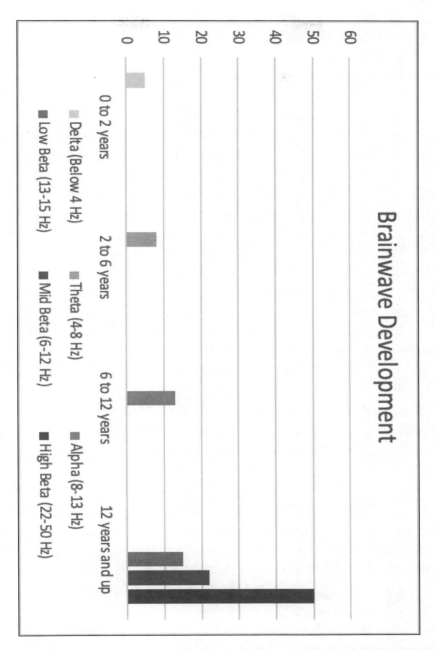

Any subtle innuendo of conditional love in childhood becomes ingrained in the brain and manifests as limiting beliefs in adulthood, such as:

I am not good enough.
I am not lovable.
I do not matter.
I have no choice.
I am not worthy.

Our parents' disapproval of us when we didn't meet their expectations or their anger and frustration when we failed to comply with their orders and commands all became internalized in us as an unconscious message of *not being good enough*.

Imagine being your three-year-old self, defenseless, vulnerable, and utterly dependent on your caregivers. Can you even fathom the dramatic effect an adult's discontent might have on a child's psyche? Let alone the yelling, punishments, abandonment, and physical and emotional abuse.

Our brain is 95% programmed by the time we are seven. We are basically adult human robots. Because of the persistent nature of our mind, we have to make untiring efforts to release ourselves from the Matrix[20] and reprogram our beliefs, thoughts, and behavior for a more empowering, awakened, and liberating lifestyle.

The good news is that reprogramming is possible because of a phenomenon called neuroplasticity or the ability of the brain to change. This is what we are doing by going through the steps of P.A.U.S.E.

Shedding the Past

As awakened souls from the Matrix, our mission is to perpetually bring awareness to our unconscious patterns and fear-based programs, rewiring our brain for peace, joy, and love.

Please note that reading a book and meditating every now and then will not accomplish this. We need persistent and daily practices. Remember how Carl Jung said, "Until you make the unconscious conscious, it will direct your life, and you'll call it fate"?

20   Referring to the movie, The *Matrix* where a false world has been indoctrinated in people's minds for the purpose of hiding the truth and promoting enslavement.

This is why it's critical to make our fears, past conditioning, and limiting beliefs conscious so they lose power. Consequently, our life's journey becomes a continuous shedding of our skin. As the bestselling author Jack Kornfield beautifully said, "Just as a snake sheds its skin, we must shed our past over and over again."

How do we know when to shed our skin? Who or what shows us how? The answer is our *pain*.

Byron Katie said, "Our loved ones will continue to press every button we have, until we realize what it is that we don't want to know about ourselves yet." When we feel triggered or helpless, it's as if someone unfolds a red carpet for us to dive deeper into our healing journey.

Those people and events who aggravate us show us which skin to shed and how to rise as a phoenix from the ashes of our pains. Our parents, partners, and children are no exception. As a matter of fact, the people in our inner circle are the best awakeners and teachers.

Let us look at this fantastic trigger discovery exercise from Dr. Shefali. Just keep in mind that we need to take the first two steps of P.A.U.S.E. to be able to do this amid chaos.

After pausing, breathing, accepting, and feeling our feelings, it's time to go on a discovery journey. This journey not only brings us closer to ourselves, it brilliantly and efficiently facilitates healing from past wounds and childhood conditioning. I believe this exercise is genuinely comparable to years of traditional therapy.

In the second part of the exercise, you can investigate a triggering event in your life, discover your reaction and the feeling you experience, and uncover the unconscious thought and beliefs that invoke the feeling. You can then come up with an alternative thought and belief to empower yourself to deal with the situation in a more conscious and compassionate way the next time it arises.

The Trigger Exercise

Inspired by Dr. Shefali's Work

I get triggered when_____

_____

_____

I get triggered because _____

_____

Because... because... (Go a few layers deep like you are peeling an onion or uncovering the next Russian doll. Start your sentences with I, not he/she or they.)

_____

_____

_____

The experience makes me feel

_____

I remember I felt like this as a child when

_____

_____

Here is an example from my life at the beginning of my conscious parenting journey.

- I *get triggered* when my kids do not pick up their laundry off the floor when I have asked them only a few hundred times.

- *Because* I am afraid they will not grow to be responsible adults.
- *Because* I feel like a nag and an incompetent mom, I did not teach them well.
- *Because* it makes me *feel* like I have no control.
- *I* remember I experienced a similar feeling as a *child* since I was always expected to be perfect, proper, and responsible. I barely remember feeling carefree. I distinctly remember my father used to ask me if anyone got 100% in class when I got 95%.
- It feels like my children's carefree and non-compliant spirit is making my inner child jealous. My real children have woken my inner child's weeping heart by provoking a similar feeling from the file cabinet of my suppressed memories.

There it is. I just uncovered the past wound that my children were merely poking by not listening to me. They simply peeled the band aid off of my inner child's past wound.

The root of all wounds is usually the fear of not being good enough, not being valued, not being loved, and not being accepted. In this case, I had a fear of losing control again, of not being the best, of not being approved, of being judged—this time by myself. It seemed as if I had downloaded and internalized my parents' voices in my head and unconsciously listened to them on repeat.

Notice how instead of using the moment to create meaningful connection with my children and maybe making a game out of doing laundry, I created a chasm between us by my:

1. *Thoughts* – "I thought I had raised irresponsible and spoiled children."

2. *Beliefs* – "I believed they should have listened to me as a parent as a result of cultural conditioning and the traditional view of parenting."

3. *Fears* – "I was afraid they would never make good choices."

4. *Past pains* – "I remembered I did not have too many choices or dominion over my life as a child, the same way I had no control over my children and my house as an adult.

5. *Feelings* – "I felt out-of-control, powerless, unworthy as an individual and incompetent as a parent."

This exercise should illuminate the fact that *nothing outside of us can hurt us*. We get hurt because of a *past* wound. The only thing the current situation does is rekindle the same emotional response from an unconscious memory from childhood. This helps shift the spotlight from my children to myself so that I'm less infuriated with them. It also empowers me to attend to my wounded child self and heal in the process.

In therapy sessions, this is the time when people come to the realization that their current experiences are the direct result of their parents' demeanor and behavior. This is the time when people predictably feel deeply resentful toward their parents and spend many other therapy hours learning to forgive them. However, to be able to surpass or at least shorten this phase of coerced forgiveness, let's hone into the keyword *choice* again.

Understanding human psychology and brain indoctrination should clear up the illusion that our parents actually had a *choice*. Like the baby elephant, they were the subject of decades of heavy programming. Unless they devoted time for some serious inner work, they were the product of habits and familial, cultural, and societal conditioning.

It's a question of realizing that our parents did the best they could according to their beliefs and defense mechanisms. They were simply incapable of doing otherwise because they too had no choice but to operate from their inner children's protective mechanism.

Remember, *we cannot expect a cat to bark.*

If we have the intention and are devoted to our practice, this book will assist us in rewiring our behavioral, mental, and emotional programming. Any other scenario is equivalent to the analogy of the cat and the dog.

While it's futile to expect our caregivers to change or even to fully grasp the gravity of the consequences of their actions, it's important and psychologically healthy to communicate our pain to our caregivers in a way that has the least cost. We can visualize them in our mind and tell them all our heart desires in such a way that the cathartic process can finally empower us to fully accept them and even cultivate compassion for their pain.

We can also journal our conversation. Please use this space to get started. Without forgiveness, we let the past steal our present.

As a famous saying goes, "Holding a grudge is like drinking poison and waiting for the other person to die." This is a good time to unshackle ingrained resentment. It's time for radical emancipation.

My Letters to My Parents

To my mother: _____

_____

_____

_____

_____

_____

_____

To my father: _____

_____

_____

_____

_____

_____

Breaking the Unconscious Cycle

Sometimes our interpersonal relationships, financial, and health situations fall into an unconscious and cyclical pattern. Someone does or doesn't do something, or an event occurs, and we get triggered because of our expectations, beliefs, fears, our impulse to control, and our resistance to the as-is of the situation. However, instead of pausing, accepting the as-is, and feeling our feelings, we react by going to the fight-flight-freeze mode, which consequently shames everyone involved and exacerbates the situation.

We are now trapped in an unconscious cycle, with no way out until we choose to pause, breathe, accept, and move through our feelings to reactivate our higher brain. Like the grown elephant, if we don't break this cycle, we remain the prisoner of our primitive fight-flight-freeze mechanism and perpetuate our power struggle with people and events indefinitely.

Even if we manage to stop the behavior in the short run by using coercion and fear, we will experience a future manifestation of the exact cycle in similar settings since we didn't attend to the root of the problem. They say, "the way we do one thing, we do everthing."

146

Deconstructing the Ego

Ego has various meanings in different settings. In this context, ego is another name for the unconscious defense mechanism or the fight-flight-freeze system. This mechanism was built for a reason in childhood. We all needed it in order to survive. We were all at the mercy of our caregivers. We had no choice but to adjust to their needs, or we were punished in some way. We either learned to fight or rebel, take flight or escape, to freeze and become numb and docile, to fawn and try to please them, or to try to fix things to avoid conflicts.

The ego is the protective shield around the inner child. This mechanism was needed for the child to be able to endure the unconsciousness of the caregivers. Ego is not "bad." It's just immature and naïve because it was built in early childhood. We needed this mechanism to survive as children to feel protected and safe. We still need it for possible *real* threats. That is why it still exists. Evolution never disposes of a bodily function that has benefits. In our household, when my children were younger, we called our ego the wolf who was always vigilant to protect us when we felt violated.

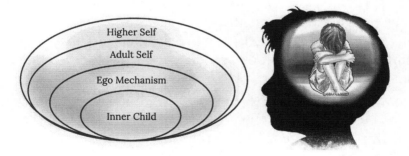

As adults it's our task to thank the ego which has served us well and ask it to sit in the passenger seat so we can be the only driver.

Our ego resides in our primitive brain. This part of the brain helped us survive the saber-toothed tigers and other prehistoric predators by elevating our heartbeat, pumping up our muscles, and producing cortisol (the stress hormone) to help us fight or flee.

147

Those were the real threats, the real life-or-death situations. That is why, even in the 21st century, when our primitive brain gets activated, the event unconsciously feels like a life-or-death situation.

The conditional love we received from our caregivers and society left our basic psychological needs unmet. Every time we were shut down, given a time out, or coerced in a hostile or judgmental way, we felt shame, and we even thought our life wasn't worth living. You read that right. We not only felt unlovable, but life felt unlivable! It sounds dramatic because it is.

The primitive brain really sucked us into a life-or-death scenario when we were little. I can certainly testify to this as I have seen it with my own kids. I remember my son, who was seven at the time, bluntly told me, "Mommy, you want me to die." He said that after I had bitterly complained he hadn't listened to me when I had asked him to do his laundry. As he grew older, he used to say, "Every time you yell at me, it feels like a piece of my heart gets ripped out." Children question their worth and their right to live when they are treated less than respectfully and compassionately.

When a boy is repeatedly punished for crying and told that *boys do not cry* , he unconsciously learns to suppress his true feelings in order to avoid punishment. As you might have guessed, this results in an adult man who isn't in touch with his feelings. As events happened repeatedly in our childhood, our protective masks became thicker and denser.

Another name for ego is the false self or the protective mask that is created out of fear. As you read about some of these mask labels that Dr. Shefali outlined below, think which mask you might be wearing. How about your partners, your kids, your parents, your colleagues, your employees, or your friends?

Here are some masks: martyr, victim, avoider, perfectionist, narcissistic, passive, busy doer, over-cheerful, over-empathetic, jokester, gambler, addict, foodie, alcoholic, shopper, procrastinator, resentful, sulky whiner, pessimist, depressive, workaholic, and pleaser.

Our job as an adult is to take off the mask of the ego, transcend the survival self, and attend to the inner child's unmet needs through connecting to our higher self, which is eternally whole, limitless, and flawless

Lighting Up the Shadows

As our caregivers perpetually strived to manipulate our feelings because our "unhappiness" made them unhappy and uncomfortable, our ego gradually developed to hide and suppress our "bad" feelings and "bad" sides. All of this was to keep our parents content and help us survive physically and emotionally. Inadvertently, we ended up transporting this fight-flight-freeze dynamic to our adulthood and unconsciously kept operating from this place, even though there were no imminent threats to our survival in adulthood. This mechanism caused a large portion of our psyche to stay suppressed and dormant within our subconscious mind, similar to an inactive volcano. Carl Jung called this repressed and unconscious part of the brain our shadow, or the unknown dark side of our personality.

Jung suggested that the shadows cause us to unconsciously project our perceived personal inferiority onto others. When we are perturbed or triggered by an event or someone's behavior, there is a high chance that we have exposed one of our shadows. We could not recognize it unless it exists within ourselves. Upon encountering and resenting our own shadow in others, our dormant volcano violently erupts and we pass unkind judgments and express rage and disappointment.

If we are aware of this dynamic, we can gracefully use people's involuntary guidance to bloom like a lotus in the mud. For this we must be truly grateful to events and people who irritate us, trigger us, and wrong us. If it were not for them, we would never know the repressed part of our psyche to integrate it. We experience fulfillment not when we feel "happy" but when we feel "complete." Uncovering our shadow empowers us to pay attention, non-judgmentally perceive them, own our "dark side," and then feel *whole*.

To do this, we must learn to cultivate radical self-acceptance and self-compassion, not *in spite of* our most despised feelings and behavior (our shadows) but *because of* them.

Although we might lash out at our loved ones, our behavior is actually a tasteless demonstration of our deep care for them. When we become agitated upon fulfilling a task, it can be an indication that we have good work ethics.

There is always a force of good even behind a wicked façade of a behavior, a feeling, or a thought. The underlying reason that gives rise to our most adverse-looking physical and psychological patterns and manifestations is still compassion-based, otherwise our self-healing psyche and immune system would not have developed it.

We must first love ourselves for our demons and shadow so we feel empowered to channel our responses in a more positive fashion. We had very little to do with their development anyway, as they were formed in our childhood to help us survive the unconsciousness of our parents, society, and culture. Then why feel guilty?

Let's see the flickering light in our shadows and let it percolate through our body, our mind, and our soul until all we see is the light of our essence, unshackled from our past conditioning. Love the wound and let the light in.[21]

Until we resist and resent our anger, our depression, our meanness, and our aggression, we are paralyzed from moving forward in our healing journey. They have been here for a reason. We must offer them our appreciation and recognition first and then release them as their services are no longer needed.

The Mask Exercise

> *"All the world is a stage, and all the*
> *men and women merely players."*
> *– William Shakespeare*

To thrive in the awakening journey, we must know our masks. When Dr. Shefali presented an eye-opening exercise in one of her annual summits in California, I was shocked that it took me several minutes to complete it. I thought I had done enough inner work and knew myself well, but it seemed the journey of healing is eternal. Please take time to do this exercise as you read.

- Please bring a blank sheet of paper to make a mask out of it by drawing two eyes, a nose, and a mouth on one side. Poke the eyes so you can see through them. You can use a real mask if you have one.

- Flip the paper and write your *needs and desires* on the back of the paper. What needs and inner desires must be fulfilled in order for you to feel happy and peaceful? For example, *I like to feel appreciated.*

---

21   "The wound is the place where the Light enters you." – Rumi

- Next, on the side that your face is on, write how you *react* when you get upset, overwhelmed, or triggered.
- Put the paper on your face like you are wearing the mask such that your needs that are on the back of the paper are touching your face and your reactions hang on the outside.
- Notice people cannot see your unmet needs behind your mask. All they see is your reactions.
- We react in defensiveness (either of fight, flight, freeze, fawn, or fix) when our needs are not met.
- For example, I get angry and try to fix everything when I don't feel appreciated. I even might flee if I feel over-whelmed.
- Remember that everyone wears a mask of their own.

This is not only how we see people but how people see us at all times. We are literally drama players with a variety of masks built in childhood that caused us to forget our true identity is made of pure light and compassion—nothing less, nothing more.

While we see the façade of rage, depression, addiction, betrayal, overpowering, and abandonment, we are blind to the unfulfilled needs beneath the mask. Although people can easily see my mask of anger, they cannot possibly recognize how my perception of feeling unappreciated has given birth to this mask. I didn't know that myself until I did the exercise. How could I possibly expect others to know?

This exercise is eye-opening. It's empowering to know that everyone is wearing these masks. It's as if we are all walking stick figures with unmet needs on the inside and with insensitive and sometimes cruel reactions on the outside. Let's remember this when we get triggered by our child throwing a tantrum, a check-ed-out spouse, or an over-critical boss.

Can you imagine taking off the mask now? Can you start re-parenting your inner child before engaging in a conflicting situation? Can you attend to her needs and soothe her in the moment by affirming that she's appreciated, worthy, enough, lovable, and that you are here to see her, hear her, respect her, and love her? After all, we are the only capable person to do this. No one else knows what's underneath our mask and no one else can truly fulfill our inner needs while they are still wearing their own mask. Who else can do that?

- Our spouse, who is not only unknowingly suffering from his or her unmet needs, but has no clue what ours are?
- Our parents? Well, they would have done it when it was their turn. Too late now.
- Our siblings, who might be wearing the rival mask?
- Our boss, who might be wearing his or her own perfectionistic and unworthiness mask?

Our kids, well, you know where I am going with this, right? I recommend watching the movie Samadhi—Maya, *the Illusion of the Self* to better absorb the phenomena of ego and a mask in a spiritual Context.

The Trigger Within

People and our circumstances mirror what needs to be healed within us. I attracted the scammers because I was already vibrating on lack and too consumed and worried about making my business thrive. I get triggered by my child's picky and unhealthy eating because I need to work on my healthy eating and curbing my own emotional eating patterns. I feel disconnected with my husband because I might be disconnected with myself and my own aspirations. I get disproportionally triggered by my children's electronic usage because I want to have more control over my life, and I unconsciously need to control them to appease my inner pain.

The fears we have about our loved ones and their lifestyles are probably the fears we have about ourselves and our own lifestyle. If we are afraid that our child will grow up to be an adult lacking self-love, the reason is we might be lacking self-confidence. Or if we are afraid they will grow up to be messy and unorganized, we might be suffering from a lack of organization in our own life. If are triggered that our spouse gets criticized by their boss, we may unconsciously question our own self-worth.

The triggers are always within us. People and events always trigger a past program within our psyche that needs to bubble up and heal. For example, I get triggered when I'm in a hurry. When I investigated the cause and the corresponding programming, I discovered that this is because of my perfectionism. Since then, I embarked on recovering from this past conditioning. I'm now a perfectionist in recovery.

To illustrate, I leave stuff around the house on purpose so my eyes get used to a little bit of mess. Yes, I was that person who used rulers to draw the lines in the mathematical fractions or make my books line up impeccably on the bookshelf. My books are still ordered from tall to short, but no more rulers.

Do not judge me; change is a journey, not a destination. I now know that perfectionism is a program I acquired from my dad. I not only learned it from his lifestyle, but I was also expected to be perfect at whatever I did as a child.

Another scenario that pushed my buttons was when my children were not on their best behavior in public. This program was triggered because of the *fear of judgment*, as I remember I always felt judged by my dad. We live in a small city. I used to think, "What if my clients or students see us and judge me or even ridicule me and know what a hypocrite I am because I can't create peace within my own family?"

I used to have a magnet on my car that said, "Mindful Living Conscious Parenting." Do you know how much pressure this exerted on me as I thought about how people might hear me yell or see my children fighting in the car? I forgot that conscious parenting is about well-behaved parents, not well-behaved kids!

Please use the next worksheet to list all your chronic emotional triggers. Get familiar with them. Investigate your subconscious thoughts, fears, feelings, and a possible associated childhood memory linked with each trigger.

Think of a strategy you can take on for each scenario to prime your brain for a preemptive plan when conflicts arise. This situates you in a place of empowerment. You are now in charge.

Take the position of the director of your inner terrain and consequently the outer dynamics.

You have now been given an opportunity to rewire your behavioral patterns, choose a different response, and co-create your reality with intention and dominion.

List Your Triggers with Associated Thoughts, Fears, Feelings, Childhood Memories, and Possible Strategies

Triggers with parents:

_____

_____

Triggers with partners:

_____

_____

Triggers with children:

_____

_____

Other interpersonal triggers:

_____

_____

Financial triggers:

_____

Health triggers:

_____

Re-Parenting and Healing the Inner Child

When we take off the mask of the ego, we see our inner child hidden behind the walls of our survival self. Our adult self can now tend to the inner child with the assistance of our Higher Self or inner guru.

Our Higher Self is the gentle, wise, always benevolent and intact part of us that hasn't lost touch with our true and compassionate essence regardless of our harsh human experiences. It's our inner knowingness, our connection to the Source, our imperishable awareness, and the bridge between our human body and our spirit. This is the Self that needs our quiet and stillness to emerge.

After pausing, accepting the as-is of the situation, attending to our immediate human feelings, and invoking our Higher Self, we are ready to address the needs of our inner child. The goal is to make her feel seen, appreciated, divinely loved, and unconditionally accepted.

There are daily activities that can help us preemptively take care of our inner child. Firstly, we must make sure we perpetually release fear, guilt, and shame throughout the day. Our inner child always imagines it isn't good enough and that it's our job to assure them that they have nothing to worry about. Communicate with your inner child like you talk to a real person.

This might seem awkward at first, but it works magic. Ask her various questions and foster reassurance and safety with your words. You can say:

- I'm sorry you're feeling (fill in the blank: unloved, unsafe, powerless, incompetent, lonely, overwhelmed).
- I'm here for you.
- You don't have to worry about anything anymore.
- You are perfect just the way you are.
- You don't have to do anything or be anything other than the amazing self you are.
- Go play. I've got this.
- I love you.

Furthermore, fill up your self-care bucket during the day by taking the time to do what brings you and your inner child joy, eat well, rest well, move well, sit in silence, and be okay with saying "no." Spending at least ten minutes in daily meditative practices is also essential to maintain the nourishment of our inner terrain.

Besides these preemptive exercises, there are some brief practices that can foster self-care and nurture our inner child. The most obvious one is to attend to the feelings of the inner child as mentioned in the second step of P.A.U.S.E. We must allow ourselves to grieve, otherwise our inner child relives heavy emotions repeatedly.

Another example is verbally or mentally reciting various mantras, such as *HAM SA* (I am That), using HAM on the in-breath and SA on the out-breath or *OM NAMAH SHIVAYA* (I bow to my Inner Self). These are wonderful portals through which we can center ourselves and revel in the inner light of our heart. By repeating both mantras, we transcend the small self and identify ourselves with the cosmos or the omnipresent divine consciousness.

As mentioned previously, Ho'oponopono, a Hawaiian practice of reconciliation and forgiveness, is also a powerful clearing technique that can be used specifically for the inner child. You simply repeat these phrases as many times as you can, either out loud or in your mind:

- Thank you
- I love you
- Please forgive me
- I am sorry

You can tell these to your inner child. You are telling her how sorry you are that she is experiencing these hard feelings. You thank her, assure her that you love her, and ask for her forgiveness repeatedly until you feel at ease. You can say these sentences to yourself while looking into your eyes in the mirror.

You can also print a photo of yourself when you were a child, look into her eyes, and commune these cathartic phrases with her with tenderness and love until you sense her peace.

You can use this tool whenever you find yourself feeling adverse feelings. This is a sign that your inner child is feeling hurt. You feel irritated by traffic; use Ho'oponopono. You feel victimized by your illness; use Ho'oponopono. You feel attacked by your boss; use Ho'oponopono. You feel triggered by your teenager; use Ho'oponopono. You feel neglected by your partner; use Ho'oponopono. You get the pattern. The tool works wonders.

Put your hands on your heart, drop from your brain to your heart, take three deep breaths into your heart, and simply ask yourself what can be done at this moment to release suffering and feel at ease. You can ask, "What's needed now?" If you have fully dropped to your heart zone, believe it or not you will hear an answer within a few seconds. Please refer to the fifth step of P.A.U.S.E. for more self-nourishing exercises and tools.

One of the ways to liberate yourself and release resentment, expectation, and frustration is to become aware of the hurt inner child of the other person. Remember that their inner child is also re-experiencing a trauma associated with their childhood. You can use Ho'oponopono for their inner child as well.

Please use this space to write messages to your inner child, your ego defense mechanism, your adult self, and your Higher Self. Sit in silence for a few minutes and start writing. Don't pick up your pen from the paper. Keep writing without overthinking and censoring yourself. This is called conscious journaling. Use separate paper if you want to keep writing.

My Letters to Myself

To my inner child: _____

_____

_____

_____

To my ego defense mechanism: _____

_____

_____

_____

To my adult self: _____

_____

_____

_____

To my Higher Self: _____

_____

_____

_____

For this last exercise, use this space to answer the questions as if your inner child is responding. There is a catch to this exercise. Write the responses to these questions with your *non-dominant hand*. Don't judge your handwriting. It doesn't even need to be legible. Don't think with your adult brain. Let your inner child be heard. You will be surprised with your inner child's authenticity and wisdom.

Inner Child Conversation

(Write with your non-dominant hand! Do not mind your handwriting!)

I love you! Thank you for talking to me! What do you want me to call you?

_____

What makes you happy? _____

_____

What is your biggest dream? _____

_____

Is there anything that makes you feel afraid, angry, ashamed, or sad right now?

_____

What do you want to say to your parents?_____

_____

What do you want from me? _____

_____

How can I help you heal?_____

_____

What is your favorite activity? _____

_____

Revisiting Love and Fear

Love	Fear
Present	Past/Future
Formless - Heart	Form - Brain
Essence: Connection Conscious Awareness	Ego: Disconnection Past Memories
Conscious Choice	Compulsive Reaction
Abundance, Peace, Joy, Non-Judgmental Acceptance of As-Is, Discernment	Lack, Chronic Worry, Rage, Guilt, Shame, Apathy, Judgment
Growth / Creativity	Fight-Flight-Freeze / Survival
True	**False**

Yes, we are revisiting love versus fear, and rest assured we will be visiting it in the future as well. I believe the realization of the ever-present polarity of fear versus love is the key to decode the treasure map in the human journey. Nurturing awareness of how our ego tends to place us in the state of fear is paramount.

Our protective and yet naïve ego assumes that by putting us on edge and constant worry, it's actually accomplishing something. However, our adult self now knows that pointless worry is, well, pointless. If your fear propels you to take a life-affirming action, please honor it. Otherwise, dismiss it. It's a simple recipe.

Perpetually shifting from fear to love is another phenomenal tool to nurture and heal our hurt inner child. Since our ego is formed in the brain in childhood, by dropping into our heart we parent ourselves from scratch the way we truly deserve, this way we can dismantle the egoistic fear-thinking and activate our heart-based wisdom.

As mentioned before, our cells operate either on the state of growth or survival. Our 50,000 thoughts a day also vibrate on the frequency of either love or fear. We even talk or behave based on these two states.

When we are fully in the present moment sipping tea, watching ocean waves, hearing birds chirping, fostering love and gratitude, feeling a hug, and even moving through our pain non-judgmentally, we are on the love state. However, mind-wandering about the past or the future places us on the fear mode, since we are either regretting the past or worrying about the future.

It isn't redundant to emphasize that love dwells in the heart and fear resides in the neural defensive network of our brain. Abundance, peace, joy, and non-judgmental acceptance of the moment is love. Lack, and low-vibration emotions—such as chronic worry, rage, shame, and judgment—emerge from fear. Love is awareness and begets creativity and growth. Fear embodies fight-flight-freeze. Love is true and fear is false.

Knowing these dynamics gives us permission to simply dispose of an egoistic and fear-based thought if it isn't a legitimate fear. When I discovered this epiphanic truth, I immediately connected with this quote from A Course in Miracles: "You have but two emotions, love and fear. One you made and one was given you."

Triggers as Opportunities to Heal

Similar to how Jung advised us to get to know ourselves through our irritation with others, Janet Jacobson affirmed, "If it is in my life, then it is in me. The people in our lives that push our buttons and rouse our judgments are mirroring back to us our disowned parts. How nice of them! The goal is wholeness: loving and accepting all our parts is what makes us whole."

No one or no event is an exception. Let's rise above our ego defense mechanism, P.A.U.S.E. and understand that the true reason we get triggered is that we need to heal a past wound within us and become whole again. As Robert Frost, the well-known American poet, said, "The best way out is always through."

To recap, the third step of P.A.U.S.E., understanding thoughts and triggers, prompts us to pause and investigate why we get triggered by people and events. The trigger:

- Either sheds light on our shadows—where we project our undesired attributes onto others as a twisted coping mechanism—in which case we try to embrace and accept our dark side to feel whole.
- Or it exposes our childhood wounds, in which case we must attend to our wounded inner child and make her feel seen and safe.

This way, we pave the path to the next step of P.A.U.S.E.

Let's dig in and un-trap our three-year-old inner child from our 40-year-old body. Let's look at these triggers as blessings, opportunities, divine guidance, and a "place where the Light enters us." Wow, is this not a captivating shift in viewpoint? The next chapter will go deeper into shifting and broadening perspectives.

Notes for the Third Step of P.A.U.S.E.

Understand Thoughts and Triggers

My takeaways:

_____

_____

_____

_____

_____

_____

What do I commit to do **every day** to understand my triggers and empower myself to take the third step of P.A.U.S.E. (Uncover childhood memories, shadow work,...)?

_____

_____

_____

_____

_____

CHAPTER SIX
FOURTH STEP OF P.A.U.S.E.: SEARCH FOR DIFFERENT PERSPECTIVES

One day, Mullah Nasreddin, the 13th-century Sufi satirist, was asked by a man to judge a complaint the man had against his neighbor. The Mulla listened to him carefully and ruled, "Yes, you are absolutely right."

The other person also went to him. The Mulla listened to his defense carefully as well and said, "Yes, you are absolutely right."

The Mulla's wife, who had heard both conversations, complained, "Both men cannot be right."

The Mulla then said, "Yes, you are absolutely right."

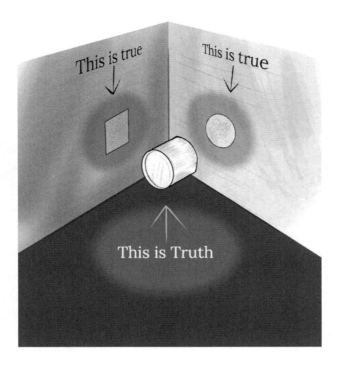

As the shadow of a cylinder is a rectangle on one wall and a circle on the perpendicular wall, we each religiously believe our perspective is the absolute truth. However, the truth is neither.

Whenever I see my loved ones or my clients entangled in the trap of judgment, I remind them that they only see their own rectangle, not the other person's circle. Reminding them they have a choice to see others' perspectives not only makes them feel good about themselves but about others. After all, *everyone is absolutely right* as the Mulla wittingly portrayed.

The first three steps of P.A.U.S.E. empower us to understand how every thought we think, every steadfast belief we believe, every infinitesimal action we take, and every unyielding judgment we rule is the result of our deep-seated brain wiring and familial, cultural, and societal conditioning. If this truth is settled, how can we possibly expect people to view the world like us? Comprehending the immeasurable depth and gravity of our widely diverse worldviews has been, by far, the most eye-opening, revealing, and epiphanic realizations I have had since the beginning of my awakening.

We not only have different perspectives, we live in different worlds. We may not even see the same color identically. Yes, I do believe this discrepancy sounds dramatic. The fascinating point is that we barely recognize this until we do some serious self-reflection and interpersonal research. We just simply expect others to understand like us, analyze like us, and have the same brain physiology, value systems, belief systems, and logic. Even mainstream science is not entirely unbiased.

To take this even further, I don't believe anyone knows the absolute truth. We simply see a version of the truth according to our psychological lenses and programs. When we have an experience, our brain searches for similar memories and experiences from the file cabinet of our past and rules out a judgment based on the previously stored knowledge in our brain. I am sure you agree that not even twins have similar file cabinets. Then why do we futilely expect others to see eye to eye with us?

Rumi beautifully depicted the limits of individual perception in the Masnavi story of "The Elephant in the Dark." As a group of men touched different parts of an elephant in the dark, they widely differed in their opinion of what the object could be.

As he was touching the trunk, one man was persistent that it was a drainpipe. As he was touching the ear, another believed it was a fan. Another assumed it was a pillar as he touched the leg, and someone else thought it was a throne as he was touching the back. Rumi continued, if any of them carried a candle, they would've been able to see the truth and settle their differences.

In the fourth step of P.A.U.S.E., we try to find a fresh new perspective in *every* situation—and I do mean *every* situation. This allows us to question our thoughts, which are mostly fear-based and hence most likely lies.

This entails the process of separating our identity from our beliefs and thoughts. I argue with the most definite conviction that most of our assumptions are probably incorrect in so many situations. So let us have a super open mind in this chapter.

Imagine a friend is not returning your calls. What's the first thing you would speculate about this situation? Let me tell you what usually happens in our brain. It keeps looking for reasons that our friend might be upset with us or doesn't care about us. Or it might worry that something bad has happened. At any point in time, there exists a myriad of causes for any event. For example, in this situation, she might have broken her phone and is in the process of purchasing a new one.

Among all these likelihoods, our brain usually finds the worst-case scenario and sticks with it. We assume the worst and believe it. Why? Because, as we have learned, our ego is programmed to keep us safe. This is its main job. In this step of P.A.U.S.E., our chief objective is to override this mechanism in a conscious way.

When it comes to interpersonal relationships, a good portion of the reason for heartbreaks and broken communications is that people basically talk in different languages due to their enslavement to their rigid perspective and stubborn fear-thinking. We simply don't know how to communicate, especially when there is a conflict. Instead of communicating our needs, we resort to criticism and wanting the other person to think differ-ently, which in turn shuts down all effective communication and gives rise to arguments.

As we discussed, we see the world with our highly exclusive and individualized lens and communicate with a false expectation that people view the world exactly like us. This is the most dire mistake we can make.

One of the epiphanic realizations that can help us release ex-pectations and suffering is that our words get lost in translation. As mentioned previously, most of our words, spoken or written, either don't get read or heard, get misread or misheard, or are widely misinterpreted, leaving us brutally vulnerable and dependent on people's power of discernment.

Trying to comprehend other's perspectives and making sense of their past experiences and childhood wounds doesn't only liberate us from internalizing people's projection on us but helps us cult-ivate compassion for those with even the most atrocious conduct and harshest judgments.

If we can recite this alchemic mantra with our heart and grit, we magically dissolve the toughest interpersonal conflicts: "I would do exactly the same if I had the same belief system, upbringing, brain wiring, and childhood trauma."

Hurt People Hurt People

Realizing that hurt people hurt people has the potential to transform our judgmental and one-sided view of almost all behaviors. This is our motto in our family, especially when it comes to bullying.

Carl Jung said, "The healthy man does not torture others—generally it is the tortured who turn into torturers."

Another radical statement that has equal potential to alter our perspectives about people is, "What's not love is a cry for love."

Aside from alleviating the negative effects on the person who is the target of the bully, believing these statements brings awareness and compassion for the bully. Several years ago, one of my son's friends was less than kind to him. My son, who was nine years old at the time, was devastated and started feeling bad about himself.

I reminded him that *hurt people hurt people.* I told him the boy might have older siblings that may treat him similarly at home. I also added the affirmative statement, "Do not take things personally."

Knowing my son, I assured him the boy's behavior had nothing to do with him. Later that week, when I was on my son's field trip, I was talking to the boy's mom when she organically mentioned how her son's older brothers were insensitive toward him at home and she was concerned that her son might have treated my son unjustly.

I have to confess that I was secretly rejoicing about my insight. When I told my son about my conversation with the mom, his eyes sparkled. It was reassuring for both of us to see how this "hurt people hurt people" phenomenon is actually true!

Knowing this empowers us to be more mindful of the way we treat our loved ones, given that our behavior will have a direct impact on how they treat others. Believe it or not, most sibling rivalries form because of this. My daughter treats my son harshly as soon as she feels hurt by me.

When it comes to children, we must constantly ask ourselves what we are teaching them in the moment. Are we okay if they do unto others what we do unto them?

If you yell when you are frustrated, are you okay if your children yell at younger siblings or friends in school when they are frustrated? Or would you rather have them regulate their emotions and respectfully find win-win solutions? Let us remember that our children learn through our behavior, not our words. Be it to teach it!

Similarly, if we expect compassionate and respectful behavior from our partner, our colleagues, and other people in our circle, we must first be vigilant about how compassionate and respectful we are toward them.

Behavior is a Symptom

Other fantastic mantras that can help us take a fresh perspective when people misbehave are "behavior is a symptom" or "behavior is a form of communication."

When we grasp this, we transcend behavior and become adamant to discover the underlying reasons behind the symptom.

We see the behavior as the tip of the iceberg sitting on a heap of unmet needs and low-vibration emotions such as: Am I loved? Am I worthy? Am I safe? Am I being heard? Can I do this? Do I matter? Do I have a choice? Do I belong?

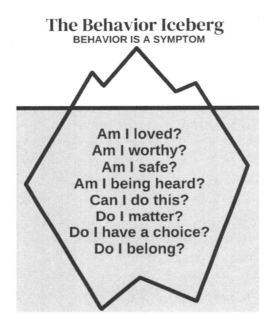

The Behavior Iceberg
BEHAVIOR IS A SYMPTOM

Am I loved?
Am I worthy?
Am I safe?
Am I being heard?
Can I do this?
Do I matter?
Do I have a choice?
Do I belong?

When it comes to children, manipulating the bad behavior by traditional symptom management techniques such as punishing, yelling, taking away privileges, giving time outs, or bribing not only exacerbates the challenging behavior over time but creates disconnection.

Similarly in relationships, arguing, fighting, abandoning, and giving the silent treatment in hopes of manipulating our partner further damages the connection and deepens the chasm.

Punitive paradigms are taking care of a symptom and neglecting the root causes—like the conventional medical system that always tries to match a pill to suppress a symptom. Their motto is "there is a pill for every ill."

An example is cough suppressants. In a more integrated medical paradigm, we look for the reasons we cough in the first place. We try to find holistic remedies to attend to the root cause of the problem, rather than suppressing the natural defense mechanism of our wise and self-healing body which is trying to expel the infection by making us cough.

The fastest path to peace is to look beyond the behavior. Most unpleasant behavior is a cry for attention, approval, and love, and we must not take them personally. If we do take them personally, it's a sign that we have a similar wound.

How do we look beyond the behavior and recognize the underlying reasons for misbehavior?

Anger is a Wake-Up Call

Marshall Rosenberg, the founder of Nonviolent Communication, eloquently said, "Use anger as a wake-up call to unmet needs." Similar to the iceberg of misbehavior, anger also sits at the 5% tip of a humongous iceberg of unmet needs and low-vibration emotions as we saw before.

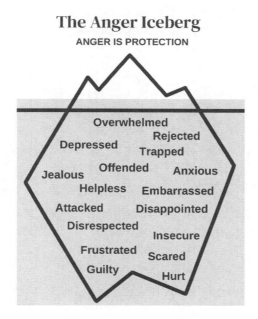

The Anger Iceberg
ANGER IS PROTECTION

Overwhelmed
Rejected
Depressed
Trapped
Jealous Offended Anxious
Helpless Embarrassed
Attacked Disappointed
Disrespected
Insecure
Frustrated Scared
Guilty
Hurt

As awakened individuals, it's our job to first heal our past wounds that people unknowingly shed light on and then cultivate self-compassion and respectful boundaries if the problem persists.

As conscious parents, it's our job to dig deep beneath our children's anger, the door-slamming, the cussing, and the hitting. We must coach them through their big feelings, attend to their unmet needs, and help them heal their wounds because they don't have the skills to do this on their own. Let's not forget that people would do better if they could.

Reasons for "Negative Behavior"

Thousands of hours of my research in the past several years have helped me to collect five specific reasons for "negative behavior." I had to use the term "negative" in this context; however, by now, we know that the polarity of human life, behavior, and mental state is confined to our human form. Let's not forget that our essence includes but is not limited to this form only. If we intend to live our whole Self, we must transcend the duality of bad or good, negative or positive, and right or wrong. Don't forget to perpetually tap into the field "out beyond the wrong doing and the right doing."

Before we move forward on this step of P.A.U.S.E., please note that while some of the content in this section is geared towards children, we can certainly generalize all the concepts to ourselves and other adults since we all have inner children trapped within our psyche that yearns for belonging and healing.

Reason #1: Neural Wiring

The number one reason for misbehavior is the state of biological responses and neurological wiring. As humans, we each have wide-apart wiring in our brain when it comes to information processing and various neurological skills.

Some research divides human intelligence into eight different types: logical-mathematical, linguistic, naturalistic, spatial, musical, intrapersonal, interpersonal, and bodily-kinesthetic. That is why it's crucial to remember that every human operates on their own term and the term of their brain, and it's simply futile to *expect a cat to bark*!

Awareness about brain capabilities and neurological skills is drastically more important when it comes to children. When a two-year-old child hurts a playmate because he kicked down his tower, it means his brain is simply incapable of communicating his frustration any other way. The human brain doesn't fully developed until the mid 20s.

It is simply unreasonable to expect children to understand others' physical and emotional pain when they don't even have the hardware in their brain. They are basically incapable of feeling empathy toward others, especially when they are in the middle of a tantrum or in a fight-flight-freeze reaction.

Dr. Siegel affirmed, "Kids misbehave because they can't control their emotions and bodies, not because they won't." This is due to the lack or incomplete development of the part of the brain that handles understanding, empathy, morality, or self-control. This is the portion of the brain that develops last.

As we saw before, as adults we are also barely able to fully grasp people's pain and cultivate empathy for them, especially in the midst of a conflict. The reason is that our protective responses to outside stimuli are mainly neurologically and physiologically built in, especially if we have not made any rewiring attempts.

As Dr. Siegel explains, we have downstairs and upstairs brains that are connected with a staircase. The most primitive roles such as breathing and fight-flight-freeze are performed in the downstairs, while upstairs deals with more evolved functions such as decision-making, problem-solving, empathy, morality, self-understanding, and control over the emotions and the body.

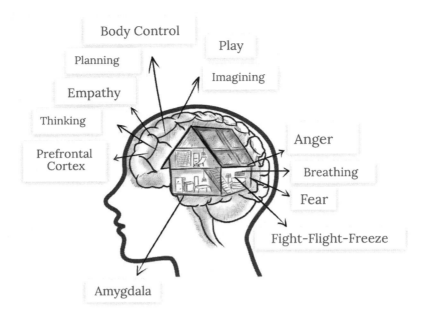

Body Control
Play
Planning
Imagining
Empathy
Thinking
Anger
Prefrontal Cortex
Breathing
Fear
Fight-Flight-Freeze
Amygdala

When we are in the fight-flight-freeze mode, the staircase is broken. That is why we need to take the first step of P.A.U.S.E. to bring the staircase back online. We must make an effort to drop our strong urges to fix, rationalize, teach, and lecture people during these times as our words cannot even be heard since the upstairs brain is offline. When it comes to children, it's best to try to connect with them emotionally, create a space, and usher them through their feelings.

Why is it important to connect to feelings within ourselves and others when the fight-flight-freeze system takes over? Because during this time, the left brain responsible for cognitive abilities is shut down. Words cannot be processed, lessons cannot be learned, and reasoning cannot be comprehended until the amygdala (the alarm brain) is deactivated and the thinking brain is back on.

These are the times we need to take the back door and use the right brain to communicate via emotional connection. This is because connection produces oxytocin, serotonin, and opiate (happy hormones) and blocks cortisol (a stress hormone). This allows us to resurrect ourselves from the fear state and be able to think with our higher brain.

Cultivating connection at these moments includes validating people. When it comes to children, offering an open heart and cultivating a safe haven for them is imperative so they can process their heavy emotions without feeling guilt and shame.

When we create a safe space for young people's emotional processing, we are letting them know that it's okay to sometimes feel yucky, reassuring them that they are still loved no matter how bad they feel. They are not bad because of their bad feelings. All feelings are valid and legitimate. We are humans after all, not machines.

LEFT BRAIN

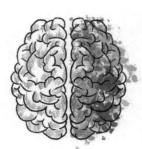

RIGHT BRAIN

Logic
Reason
Words
Control
Practicality

Love
Intuition
Peace
Freedom
Creativity

When we choose to accept our children's hard emotions without judgment, we are practicing and teaching the valuable lesson of impermanence—the aphorism that *this too shall pass.* Handling feelings this way prevents them from transforming into toxic emotions in the future. When it comes to our children, we are saving them future therapy fees—maybe not entirely, but to a great extent.

The keyword is *connection:*

- Connection begets cooperation.
- Connection before correction.
- Connection heals.
- Connection is the building block of the human brain.

- Lack of connection is the root cause of addiction.

By connecting to ourselves and others, we dismantle our fight-flight-freeze mechanism. We are able to comprehend the underlying reasons behind people's behavior. Also, we are able to tap into our higher brain and inner wisdom to take the next step with love, compassion, and grace.

Reason #2: Unmet Basic Physical Needs

The second reason for misbehavior is the unmet basic physical needs, such as food, sleep, shelter, and safety. This awareness allows us to create more patience and compassion for ourselves and others when we are tired, hungry, or sleepy.

In Maslow's hierarchy of needs[22], physiological and safety needs have to be satisfied first in order for the individual to move up to the next stages of love and esteem. Once all those needs are satisfied, the level of self-actualization can help achieve our potential. Having preemptive measures to fulfill these needs on a regular basis is crucial if we are to elevate the quality of our life and wellbeing. This is where self-care transcends selfishness and becomes essential.

Reason #3: Unmet Basic Psychological Needs

The next underlying reason for misbehavior is unmet basic psychological needs. This is based on my favorite academic theory, the Self-Determination Theory (SDT). According to the developers of this theory, Edward Deci and Richard Ryan, who have researched extrinsic and intrinsic motivation for decades, the three psychological needs of competence, autonomy, and relatedness or connectedness motivate the self to initiate healthy behavior.

The fulfillment of these needs is essential for psychological health and wellbeing. These needs are said to be universal, innate, and psychosomatic. We can look at these needs as three

---

22   Maslow's hierarchy of needs is a theory in psychology proposed by Abraham Maslow in his paper, "A Theory of Human Motivation."

buckets that need to be filled to their capacity every day for the person to thrive.

Although it was our caregivers' job to fill up these buckets in childhood, as adults we are responsible for filling them ourselves. As our unconscious parents did their best, we need to forgive their failings. It's also important not to impose this responsibility on our partners, as they have their own empty buckets to fill. Let's get on with fulfilling our own needs on a daily basis so that we are able to live our fullest potential and experience the joy that has been our inherent birthright all along.

When it comes to our children, we are fully responsible for filling up their buckets, especially before they are six years old. After six, we are still fully in charge, but part of our responsibility is to coach them on how to do it for themselves.

I like the analogy of depositing into our children's bank account when we fill their buckets, as well as withdrawing from the account when we yell, punish, or ask them to do things they are not willingly ready to do. Dr. Seigel warned, "You cannot teach children to behave better by making them feel worse. When children feel better, they behave better."

When all these needs are met, the person is intrinsically motivated to cooperate and accomplish tasks. Furthermore, they feel fulfilled and experience greater wellbeing.

Basic Psychological Need #1: Connectedness

The first need is relatedness, connectedness, or connection. Relatedness is the need to feel loved, connected, belonged, and cared for. When this need is fulfilled, it feels like we have meaningful relationships and interactions with other people. Connection is the crucial factor in the wellbeing of humans. Research shows that lack of connection is the cause of addictive behavior.

It's critical to know that connection or love is the building block of the human brain. Connection produces oxytocin (the cuddle hormone) as well as serotonin, which is the contributor to feelings of wellbeing and happiness. These hormones are cortisol blockers, which is the stress hormone. Connection takes us out of the fight-flight-freeze system and reactivates our thinking brain. The hormones released by connection make people mentally healthy and happy from inside out, and they make children smarter and more emotionally resilient. Last but not least, *connection begets cooperation,* which is one of my favorite mantras.

When we ask something of another person without connecting to them on a deeper level, we are violating their sense of autonomy, which is the second psychological need. There are three ways to gain cooperation from people: fear, bribe, or connection. The first two ways are, of course, unconscious and wreak havoc in the psyche of people, while the third option is the only conscious route. And in the conscious route, the following four tools can create connection and cultivate cooperation:

- Play
- Humor
- Curiosity
- Validation

The bottom line is that humans are gravely lacking relatedness and connection at every level. We aren't connected with ourselves, with each other, and with nature. That is why it's essential to spend at least ten minutes sitting in silence in order to become friends with our own inner terrain.

This is an opportunity to watch our thoughts as they arise and detach from them as we become aware of them. This persuades our analytical mind that we are not our thoughts and are merely the witness observing them. It empowers us to disidentify from our fear-thinking and tap into our whole Self, our intact essence. By watching our thoughts, feelings, and sensations come and leave, our true nature becomes available to us. Once we quiet our restless mind, our cosmic limitless consciousness stands within reach.

Spending at least 15 minutes in nature daily, especially barefoot, is a great way to foster a connection to ourselves and nature. While these activities foster individual inner connection, humans need one-on-one human contacts, undivided attention, and unconditional love on a daily basis. People do better when they feel better, and we feel better when we are connected to ourselves and others.

The following paragraphs revolve around some conscious parenting tips. However, I urge you to keep reading even if you are not a parent. Keep in mind that you are re-parenting your inner child even if you are not a parent to a real child, and these tips can come in handy. I have intertwined some tips for adults in this section.

There are some daily routines that we can do to fill up our children's connection bucket on a consistent basis. Firstly, use most of your words throughout the day to encourage your children and show them love. You can use this tip for your partner too. Don't praise children because of their behavior or tasks. Such may unwillingly foster *conditional* love. Instead, describe their work, encourage their efforts and kind behavior, and be a loving observant.

In this section, I would first like to talk about the 80-20 rule. You can apply this rule to your partner and other people in your close circle. Parents' words and behaviors should feel good to the child 80% of the time. Nevertheless, the average parent gives 90% negative to 10% positive attention.

Positive attention includes unconditional acceptance, admiration, positive feedback, showing a good mood, singing, dancing, playing, kissing, hugging, empathic mirroring, and being present. Negative attention may entail lecturing, teaching, arguing, raising your voice, and saying no. Going back to the bank account example, we can consider positive attention as depositing into people's bank account and negative attention as withdrawing.

Considering the magic ratio of 80-20 and the fact that we have trapped inner children within us, notice how you talk to your partner, colleagues, parents, siblings, and friends. How about yourself? How do you talk to yourself throughout the day?

Cultivate cognizance of your words with others as well as your self-critical *ANTs*. Make a conscious effort to use encouraging and empowering words for yourself and people you come in contact with.

How about this? Let's make an effort to talk less in general. Let's go on a word-fast by decreasing our words to 70% throughout the day, speak only if what we have to say is positive, and articulating the negative with a positive twist. Challenge yourself to start your sentence with a *yes* even if you need to say *no*.

For example, "Yes, you're right. That's a legitimate perspective. Here is what I think about it…" When we say *no*, we shut down open communication and place the other person in a defensive mode. Hearing the word *yes* calms their nerves and increases their receptivity. Word-fasting allows our brain to more carefully examine the words that need to be said because they are now precious commodities.

A vital practice to cultivate connection during a tantrum or anxiety is *empathetic word mirroring* accompanied by *affect matching*. Use your mental faculty to truly observe life from other people's perspectives and make them know you recognize their pain by mirroring their desires, their words, their feelings, and their affects. This works wonders. As we see later, one of humans' basic needs, and maybe the most fundamental need, is to be *seen*. Empathic mirroring takes care of this. Just be careful that you are genuine in your empathy. Energy speaks louder than words.

When it comes to children, there are some activities that can be systematically done throughout a day to preemptively fill their connectedness bucket. One of the most powerful practices is spending a ten-minute one-on-one with each child every day. Younger children will need two ten-minutes during the day. Rough housing, playing ball, racing, jumping, dancing, singing, pillow fights, playing tag, building forts, drawing, and playing with toys are some of the activities that can be done together during this time.

Here are some guidelines for one-on-one time:

- Announce it's "Mommy-Ariana time."
- Set a 10-minute timer together or let them do it.
- Sit at eye-level with your child.
- Have no agenda. Let them decide. The only thing they cannot pick is digital screening.
- You can ask, "What do you want to do for our special time?"
- If they don't want to do anything, be present with them. Become cognizant of the electromagnetic field around your heart.
- Just sit in their vicinity and watch them play with their toys or draw until they want to engage with you.
- Cultivate feelings of love and compassion.
- Kiss them your eyes.

Please allocate at least one ten-minute alone time with yourself and one ten-minute one-on-one time with your partner every day. Do you ever buy a plant and not water it? When we fail to take care of a plant, it ultimately dies. Our interpersonal relationships are like plants. They will wither and die if left unattended.

The next practice to fill up the connection bucket is to give 20-second hugs after each separation period in the morning and after school. I used to sit on the floor with open arms when my kids came through the door from school and announced, "Time for 20!" That was the time I cherished the most. Know that they will enjoy it too even if they pretend not to. This practice makes children feel special and genuinely seen, which shows them that they matter. We can do this forever, even when they are 50.

Research shows keeping the hug for 20 seconds makes the body produce oxytocin or the happy hormone. Go ahead and give 20-second hugs to all your family members and beyond.

With your partner, be adventurous and try 20-second French kisses every day. If anyone says you are being weird, tell them it's for the sake of science. I am cautioning you that both the hug and the kiss might feel awkward at the beginning, but persevere.

Consistent practice maintains the happy hormone level and creates deep and meaningful connections between people.

The next practice that I absolutely savor is the nighttime snuggle with children, as well as with partner. I snuggle with each of my kids for five to ten minutes in their beds. I scratch their backs and whisper in their ears how much I love them and how awesome they are. I hug them tight and pour my heartfelt love onto them like there is no tomorrow. To be honest, this is the highlight of my day. It feels like I vibrate on 1,000 on the Scale of Consciousness. This is the time that creative ideas pour in.

Another fantastic daily practice is to spend five minutes of laugh-time with your family. Tell jokes, do pillow fights, dance to silly music, and jump and move in a goofy and childlike manner. Be creative. This is a great time for you to be a kid all over again. Take advantage of this time to heal your inner child. Do it for you, not only for them.

Here is a fantastic mindfulness game that you can play with your family at the dinner table, after school, or at your family meetings to cultivate connection. The game is called *Rose, Bud, Thorn*. Start with yourself, and then each member of the family gets a turn.

- *Rose* is an enjoyable event during the day.
- *Bud* is an act of kindness that you did or observed.
- *Thorn* is a mistake you made. Just make sure everyone mentions what they *learned* from their mistake and how they *repaired* it.

When my kids don't have a *thorn*, I say, "What a boring day!" This implants the idea in them that it's okay to make mistakes and is part of being human. This is how we grow, become resilient, and don't easily lose our sense of wholeness and wellbeing. This can contribute to releasing the program of perfectionism and feelings of unworthiness. It also strengthens the skill of problem-solving and the importance of mending the conse-quences of our choices.

Now that we are on the topic of making mistakes, it's important that we genuinely apologize to our children and other loved ones for our own thorns on a daily basis. This is not an apology: "I am sorry that Mommy yelled, *but* I felt frustrated after asking you ten times to pick up your backpack." Apologize with *no buts.* Confess that unconsciousness took over.

Children, especially younger than six, unconsciously idolize their parents, assume they are flawless, and usually feel lesser than them. This is because they see their considerably larger and older caregivers as their sole source of survival. Apologizing shifts this perspective and assures them that they are just as valuable and important. It also eliminates the false belief that parents are flawless and all-knowing creatures with superpowers. They see that they are souls with equal value and dignity who make mistakes just like themselves. In fact, parents are probably more confused and powerless than children are.

Dr. Siegel's four Ss of attachment parenting can be another fantastic approach to look at the connectedness phenomenon. Here they are:

- *Seen:* Perceive children meaningfully and empathically and understand the underlying reasons for their behavior to make them feel seen.

- *Safe:* Avoid actions that threaten or hurt them to make them feel safe.

- *Soothed*: Help them deal with difficult emotions and situations to make them feel soothed.

- *Secure:* Help them develop an inner sense of wellbeing to make them feel secure.

We can treat these like buckets or bank accounts. Our intention should be to help our real child, our own inner child, and the inner children of our loved ones feel *seen, safe, soothed,* and *secure.*

When it comes to adults, keep in mind that the number one person responsible to do this is ourselves.

Notice that *happy* is not in the list of four. Our job is *never* to make people *happy*, not even children if they are over 14 months old. Our sole mission is to create the space for people to move through their unhappiness without feeling shamed, judged, and unworthy. Our biggest job as conscious parents is to create conditions where our children can love themselves unconditionally.

L.R. Knost, the founder and director of the children's rights advocacy, has a beautiful way of articulating the same concept. "So many problems can be avoided if we respond in *L.O.V.E.* instead of reacting in haste."

- *Listen* - "I hear you."
- *Observe* - "I see you."
- *Validate* - "I accept you."
- *Empathize* - "I understand you."

Basic Psychological Need #2: Autonomy

The next basic psychological need is autonomy, which is the need to experience behavior as voluntary and reflectively self-endorsed.

When autonomy is fulfilled, it feels like we have control over what we do. When we constantly bark orders at our kids, our partners, and others, we are compromising their sense of autonomy. When we are constantly nagging, ordering, and complaining, we cannot expect any *yeses* from them without power struggles.

No one likes to be told what to do – no one.

When it comes to adults, we try to regulate our requests from them as much as possible. But we expect children to comply with whatever we ask of them simply because they are children and are "supposed to." Do you not think this is similar to treating someone like a slave?

Do we instantly listen to our spouse if they order us to brush our teeth now? If our answer is no, then why do we think it's natural to expect our children to do so? If we are fair, we see that we have the tendency to treat everyone like robots or slaves, especially our children.

When it comes to requests, it boils down to the energy of asking. Coming alongside people, giving them choices, and genuinely asking for cooperation has an entirely different energy than when we are nagging and unconsciously resenting why no one listens to us.

One of the ways to fulfill autonomy is to get into the habit of giving two choices in the place of every request. Here are some examples:

- To children: "Do you want to eat now or in ten minutes?"
- To children: "Do you want to make your bed now or after breakfast?"
- To partner: "Should we take the kids outside now or in ten minutes?"
- To boss: "Do you want the report now or at lunchtime?"

Offering two choices to people makes them feel they are in charge, which consequently helps their inner child feel seen, heard, autonomous, and fulfilled. Challenge yourself to rephrase all your requests in the form of two choices when you need something from someone. Be creative. Let's go for fewer words, less ordering, fewer expectations, less judgment, and more choices.

Basic Psychological Need #3: Competence

The next basic psychological need is competence. This is the need to experience our behavior as effectively enacted. When competence is fulfilled, it feels like we've done a good job.

One of the most significant longitudinal studies in Harvard has found that happy and successful adults had two things as children, *love and chores.* Personally, I prefer the words responsibilities, family work, or community work in place of chores.

This research is genius. When I see some of my most loving, patient, and conscious clients struggle with their kids, I know that this is the bucket that has yet to be filled. Of course, like every other skill, it's better to reinforce this early on, even from two years old. Be creative and try to find tasks you can allocate to each family member both individually and within the household.

For children, think of real tasks, such as washing their own dishes when they are done eating, preparing lunch boxes, folding laundry, making their own bed, making the beds of their infant siblings, dusting, vacuuming, putting out the garbage bins, watering the plants, and letting them do their schoolwork by themselves.

It's important to stop reminding your children to put their homework in their backpack. If you keep reminding them, when and how will their brain learn to do this by themselves? We do almost everything—even thinking for our kids until they are 16, 17 or 18—and then we expect them to be fully independent gurus after their 18th birthday. Skills need time to be honed. Give your children plenty of opportunities to practice from early ages.

Similarly, stop reminding your spouse to put the garbage bin out. Refrain from micromanaging every task. This prevents them from unconsciously thinking they have married one of their parents.

By allowing your family members to be their own project managers and trusting them with their tasks, we not only avoid our own energy burnout, but we are helping them feel good about themselves. According to the Harvard study, when it comes to children, we have succeeded in raising responsible kids who grow to be happy, caring, and self-driven adults.

The first time I had to leave my family for a week for my PhD residency, I did it with hesitation and a heavy heart. It was bloody hard and a radical act to surrender my perfection-oriented micromanager position to my husband. I came back home to a drastically transformed household. I started feeling less burned out as I gradually transferred a noticeable portion of my parenting tasks to my husband. This not only lightened my burdens, it offered him a tremendous dose of competence and consequently intrinsic fulfillment.

I have also solved my daughter's picky eating by allocating cooking and preparing food for herself to her. Voila!

When you request something of people, make sure the other buckets of connectedness and autonomy are full, otherwise you might encounter a power struggle. In any case, people's reaction resides in your energy. What kind of responses do you think I receive if I ask someone, "It will really help me or it will save me if you…" or if I say, "I have asked you a million times to…"?

Also, if you are wishy-washy with your requests or boundaries, power struggles can be expected. Your clear and firm but empathetic energy is the elixir to receive cooperation. Just remember connection first.

When it comes to children, join them in the task for a few minutes and then release.

Lastly, when it comes to expecting our kids to do their tasks, we must first do our portion of the job playfully, patiently, and diligently. Yelling from the kitchen isn't going to teach our kids any skills. We did not learn how to run in one attempt. First we crawled, then we attempted to walk. We stumbled and fumbled numerous times until we were able to walk, and then we ran. Here is the formula to teach a new skill:

1.   Do it for them five to ten times as they watch.
2.   Do it with them five to ten times.
3.   Watch them do it five to ten times.
4.   Then, they will do it independently.

It is essential to go through this process with radical positivity, playfulness, and humor. This ensures the task process gets programmed and associated with a pleasant memory for your children. This way, there's a greater chance they will be intrinsically motivated to attend to their responsibilities.

Even then, release expectations and let go of the result. Always maintain fresh and creative energy. Don't let your past expectations obliterate the present moment. Do not forget to P.A.U.S.E. when you get triggered.

When you or someone you know is feeling unmotivated, irritated, or disheartened, examine which of these basic psychological needs might not be met. Has the person been feeling connected to herself as well as others? Has she been in control of her life choices? Has she been accomplishing any personal or community tasks and feeling fulfilled? When it comes to children, our task as conscious parents is paramount in fulfilling these basic psychological needs, not for our children alone but for the sake of healing the generational pain of the entire planet. L.R. Knost brilliantly said, "Meeting children's doesn't create needy adults. It creates healthy adults."

Three Basic Psychological Needs

CONNECTEDNESS

When this need is fulfilled, it feels like we have meaningful relationships and interactions with ourselves and others.

- Daily 10-minute silence time
- Daily 10-minute 1-1 with loved ones
- 20-second hugs
- Snuggle time at night
- Encouragement
- Empathy

AUTONOMY

When autonomy is fulfilled, it feels like we have control over what we do.

- Less ordering
- More choices
- Family meetings
- Win-win solutions

COMPETENCE

When competence is fulfilled, it feels like we have done a good job.

- Personal and family tasks
- Community work

Reason #4: Lack of Boundaries

If we don't have a few firm but empathetic boundaries, we might co-create people's "misbehavior." This also pertains to setting boundaries for ourselves so we don't feel violated and burned out.

An effective and clear boundary originates within ourselves. For example, if we take timeouts for ourselves when we are about to lose our cool about a misbehavior, it will gently send a message to people that we don't appreciate inconsiderate and disrespectful behavior.

When it comes to parenting, people sometimes think that conscious parenting is permissive parenting. This is far from the truth. Although conscious parenting's primary tool to gain cooperation is *connection* as opposed to *fear and bribing*, boundaries are considered sacred in this style of parenting.

It's essential to know that boundaries need to be set within us. We need to have boundaries to prevent our self-care bucket from leaking. The trick is to honor and respect our boundaries ourselves, rather than expecting others to do so. People will continually test our limits until they are certain we are not being wishy-washy with our boundaries.

Once we have clear energy about our noes, everyone else will naturally accept their limits. Do you ever allow your 10-year-old drive a car? This is the energy you need to have if you're actually adamant about a no.

No matter how long we meditate, eat well, exercise, and do manicures, if we aren't clear about our boundaries and fail to consistently enforce them for the people around us, our self-care bucket will continually leak.

When my daughter used bad language, I firmly but neutrally said, "I don't like to hear that word. I just need a break to cool down and take care of my ego." This space helped me to P.A.U.S.E., so I wouldn't react and resort to punitive measures. This also allowed me to get curious about her unmet needs and respond compassionately. My mental and energetic resources were then liberated to help me talk to her about her feelings and why she felt the urge to behave this way.

There is a high probability that your traditional mind will complain, "Isn't that rewarding the negative behavior?" Know that this assumption is far from the truth and is simply a myth. Rise above this voice.

By now you know that a misbehavior emerges simply because of an unmet need. Misbehavior isn't the problem, it's the response to a problem. People will do better *if they can*. Our job is to find and fulfill the need and not deepen the pain.

By preventing my ego from dancing with hers, I created an opportunity for my daughter to think about her behavior. If I punished her, I would have lost this chance. She would have felt shamed and probably resented me for imposing pain on her by yelling or punishing her.

When we punish our children or give them timeouts, we assume they will naturally and wisely use the time to ponder, "Oh, I made such an unwise choice. I should probably make an effort to repair what I did and avoid repeating it in the future."

Unfortunately, we all know this is not the case. They probably feel resentful and confused, telling themselves, "My mom is so mean. I hate her. I hate my life. I hate myself. I hope to die." These phrases might seem dramatic, but there is a high chance this monologue occurs in their minds.

I go into more details of boundaries later. But for now, I like to mention that it's essential to have only a few nonnegotiable rules for children, three to five. Otherwise we jeopardize their need for autonomy. The examples could be brushing teeth every night or having limited digital screening.

There was a time that I laminated a paper with 30 rules! Now I am very sneaky and only have one, "*Be kind.*" This covers everything, since hygiene is a sign of being kind to one's body and no name calling is a sign of being kind to another.

Yes, I have come a long way. I am sure you can now feel the amount of confusion and frustration I had in the past years. I wish I knew these conscious parenting principles at those times.

When it comes to adult relationships, creating self-nurturing boundaries is deemed critical for personal wellbeing. We must always turn the spotlight within even when people violate our limits. It takes courage to recognize that we say yes to people not because of them but because it makes us feel good about ourselves. We say yes because we unconsciously like to feel needed. It makes us feel we matter. We feel like a provider, a pleaser, and finally like a victim

When it comes to personal boundaries, recognizing the dance of self-discipline and surrendering empowers us to perpetually act in alignment with our essence with ease, grace, joy, and flow. Creating a heart-based discipline around meditation, food, exercise, work, creative work, interpersonal relationships, personal development, and service is essential for a fulfilled life, as well as our physical and psychological wellbeing.

Reason #5: Addictive Consumption

The last reason for misbehavior is addictive consumption. This could be a side effect of a lack of boundaries, but I think it merits its own section.

While the obvious impulsive shopping, emotional eating, and substance abuse can foster habits in us, the widespread addictive attribute of electronic consumption is beyond aggravating. Since I know this is the most prominent predicament in families, this section might be heavily related to parenting and digital screening. Nevertheless, I encourage you not to skip it since adults are the subjects of technology addiction as well.

Not surprisingly, addictive screening has became an escalating problem in martial relationships as I see it for my clients. Also, some of the tips in this section can be generalized to all other addictive tendencies, activities, and substances, such as the concept of addiction iceberg and the mindfulness tool of urge surfing to surf the urge of addictive compulsions.

"Mom...one more minute, please, please, please!" If you are a parent of a young child, there is a high probability that you have heard this plea or something similar in the past several years.

We have all been caught off-guard with the advent of smartphones that incorporated mind-blowing games and entertaining social media platforms. Since we found it impossible not to when their friends all owned a smartphone, we bought one for our children. We assumed building fake architecture on an iPad would make our child smarter. We found social media platforms socially inevitable and essential for our teenage son or daughter's sense of connectedness and belonging. We gave in without sufficient knowledge about the ins and outs of what we stepped into, and now we are suffering the consequences.

Although there is an abundance of research depicting the harm digital screening imposes on our brain, our wellbeing, and our relationships, we barely recognize or refuse to acknowledge the gravity of the situation since the research is not overly publicized. Nonetheless, the technocrats, such as Steve Jobs, refused to give the iPad to his kids as he knew better.

If we probe enough, we find that research has revealed that over-dependence on technology directly impacts depression, anxiety, stress, self-esteem, loneliness, and feelings of rejection in families and has adverse health implications such as addiction.

Researchers define the negative association between psychological wellbeing and technology overuse an "iDisorder." Some findings showed a positive correlation between social media addiction and depression, revealing that depression significantly predicted social media addiction. Although online relationships on social media, games, or other platforms may seem relational, they are in no way a healthy substitute for real-life interactions, leaving the basic psychological need of relatedness unfulfilled.

The fact of the matter is that smartphones, games, social media, and easy-to-access shows are here to stay, and we should hold a positive, firm, and informed position about them, especially when it comes to our children. Nevertheless, make an effort to postpone buying smartphones as long as you can, even longer than 8th grade, and avoid portable devices or massively minimize the time for children younger than six.

Being a mother of two, helping hundreds of families, and after years of reflection, research, and consultation with experts, I have finally reached a conclusion. The following is a synopsis of how we can approach the beast in the house more consciously, wisely, and compassionately.

1. Digital screening acts like narcotics on the brain. Digital devices are intentionally designed to keep us hooked. Yes, digital screening is addictive, and the subject of addiction is *information*. With every swipe, every alert, a new text, new images, the thumbs up, the comments, a new scene, the shiny objects, the sound cues, and the fake rewards the brain perceives, we get a surge of dopamine that's commonly known as the pleasure chemical. These chemicals change our brain, training us to need more dopamine hits from the device and trap us in a feedback loop that's impossible to resist.

2. Knowing the addictive properties of digital screening, we must release our children from many unrealistic expectations. Not only must we remember that the human brain isn't fully developed until the late 20s, it's also critical to understand that children are simply not able to self-regulate their screening time by themselves. If we want them to do so, we must extensively educate them, train them to cultivate self-awareness, and teach them tools to make conscious choices to rise above the forces of addiction. Even then, they need our support. Do you trust an alcoholic with a bottle?

3. Excessive digital screening could be associated with the underlying reasons for many other family and behavioral conflicts. It's crucial to understand that being constantly on digital screening desensitizes the brain to real-life activities by making them look boring compared to the glare of the digital world. Feelings of depression, isolation, and

demotivation could all be the symptom of technology addiction. That is why it's imperative to alternate screening and non-screening activities throughout the day to prevent continuous dopamine surge. Before branding your child with various labels such as ADD, ADHD, ODD, OCD, anxiety, depression, and many more, try a two-week digital detox and see what happens. (Disclaimer: This is easier said than done, but at least it brings awareness to the situation at hand.)

4. Addiction is an activity we take on to make ourselves temporarily feel good. We usually feel lethargic, hung-over, more depressed, and exhibit withdrawal symptoms after the activity or its effects are terminated. It's crucial to have a roadmap or strategy to prevent falling into the trap after the devices are taken away.

5. The root of addiction is the lack of connection. We all have a void within us and must intentionally fill this void with positive activities and thoughts, such as meaningful interactions with others, physical exercise, meditation, creative activities, and task accomplishments. Failing to do so will leave us no choice but to resort to temporarily fill the void with negative actions that are addictive and numbing, such as alcohol, drugs, junk food, shopping, working, gossiping, and digital screening. The goal is the same, to feel good. One actively makes us feel connected, fulfilled, and overjoyed. The other numbs our pain temporarily and fabricates a false sense of belonging and feelings of relatedness. When we retrieve digital devices from our children, it's essential to replace them with a good dose of connection and high-quality activities to decrease the withdrawal symptoms. The best replacement is your presence and love. Children spell love with the word T-I-M-E, which manifests in your undivided attention and love-filled connection.

Another tool that can empower us as well as our children when it comes to compulsive and addictive behavior is *surfing the urge.* Practice looking at an application icon, a ready-to-be-checked-out shopping cart, a piece of cake, or a TV remote control and feel the urge of wanting to indulge. If you sit with the urge for twenty to ninety seconds, there is a great chance that the urge subsides and you won't need to resort to compulsively filling the void.

6. Any behavior is a form of communication and merely a symptom. As conscious parents, we must attend to the underlying needs rather than trying to manipulate or fix the behavior. Having plenty of one-on-one time with each child throughout the day is crucial to fulfilling the basic psychological need of connectedness and can possibly dissolve many forms of addictive patterns.

7. Communicate with your child about the addictive properties of digital screening. Coach them to cultivate awareness about their inner terrain. Making the connection between the feelings of inadequacy and constantly engaging on social media and interactive games is crucial. Come up with win-win solutions and a digital contract together in a family meeting. Involving them in the decision-making process ensures their sense of autonomy remains intact. Nevertheless, do not expect them to comply with your agreement by themselves. You are the enforcer and need to help them stick with the guidelines of love and affirmative energy. Release all expectations. Expectation is the root of suffering.

Sample digital contract:

*   At least ten minutes of one-on-one time with each parent
*   Physical activities (dancing, hiking, biking, various sports)
*   Creative activities (music, arts and crafts, drawing, cooking)
*   Learning new skills (language, music, fixing things around the house)
*   Reading books
*   Helping around the house and community work (to fulfill the sense of competence, which is another basic psychological need)

- Alternatively engaging in these real-life activities ensures two hours of digital screening (preferably spread out throughout the day)
- Sample consequence: Loss or decreased amount of digital screening the next day if not engaged with the real-life activities mentioned in the agreement

8. Implement the guidelines with calmness, clarity, and compassion as we extensively discuss in the next step of P.A.U.S.E. A police officer doesn't yell at us while giving us a traffic ticket. Join in with their digital screening activity for five minutes. Connect with them. Ask them questions as if you are interested. When the time's up, accompany them to their next positive activity for a few minutes until they are ready to do it independently. Think of intervals, such as 30 minutes of independent time and 10 minutes of connection time. In the connection time, dance to silly music, jump on a trampoline, play tag, do a pillow fight together. Enjoy the time! Your inner child will thank you for it.

9. Increase hugs and kisses, endearing words, words of encouragement, playfulness, and humor. Decease lecturing, raising your voice, saying "no," negative comments, and excessive words to make them feel seen, loved, accepted, and safe. The lack of connection is the root of the addiction. As mentioned previously, don't be intimidated by children's boredom. Boredom not only enhances imagination and creative thinking, but it allows us to be friends with ourselves. It teaches us not to constantly look for stimuli from the outer world to make ourselves happy. Boredom is almost a meditative activity. It allows us to sit in silence and be the witness of what gracefully arises in the moment and be okay with it.

10. Be it to teach it!
- Be a good role model.
- Avoid screening unless it's necessary.
- Turn off notifications.
- Delete as many applications as you can.

- Unsubscribe from emails.
- Allocate a specific time for emails and social media.
- Avoid screening one hour after you wake up and one hour before bedtime.
- Use restricting properties of your phone for yourself as well.
- Get yourself and your family out into nature as much as you can.
- Do what you asked your children to do in the digital contract.
- Create conditions for your children to succeed.
- Every time you want to tell your children something, show courage and consider that it's something you need to say to yourself.

The Addiction Iceberg

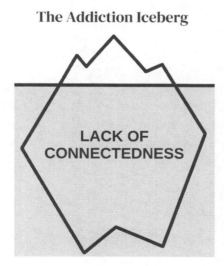

Transcending the Behavior

By taking the first three steps of P.A.U.S.E., we will be more equipped to take a compassion-based action when people need us to be the light in their darkness. We will be more empowered to see beyond their behavior when they are angry, frustrated, or out-of-control.

As we become skilled in cultivating cognizance over our thoughts and feeling our feelings, we can more cleverly investigate our triggering thoughts and try to see other perspectives.

This is important because, by now, we know that thoughts lead to feelings, and feelings lead to behaviors.

Therefore by having dominion over our thoughts, we can have dominion over our lives—specifically, how we react to our lives. Hence, it only seems logical to make it a habit to pause and scrutinize our thoughts and their legitimacy and willingly look for other viewpoints in every situation.

Let's examine a scenario. Our teenager slams the door and swears at us. What could be the thought that triggers us to get furious and frustrated in this situation?

- She's a brat!
- She's rude!
- How dare she!
- Or we target ourselves... I'm a horrible parent!
- Or the situation... this is not fair!

If we have cognizance of our thoughts, we can easily see that we're uncounsciously shooting ourselves in the foot by thinking worst-case scenarios:

- Either she's bad
- Or I'm bad
- Or the situation is bad

By taking charge of our thoughts, we can choose—and the keyword is *choose*—to look for other perspectives and think more positive or, better yet, more realistic thoughts such as:

- My teenager is frustrated and overwhelmed and doesn't know how to regulate her emotions.

- Something has happened in school, and she can't wrap her head around it.
- She feels her autonomy is violated and is fighting for it.
- She's communicating her powerlessness, loneliness, unworthiness, or other difficult emotions through her behavior.

Thinking of any of these thoughts and perspectives has the potential to bring compassion to our heart and help us be the guide our teenager needs, so we can more readily take the fifth step of P.A.U.S.E.

Going through the first four steps empowers us to take a step back and avoid reacting to a hurricane with another hurricane. By wearing our X-ray vision goggles, we can observe everyone's need to be seen, transcend all behaviors, and act according to our inner guidance and compassion. This is the recipe for liberation.

When it comes to children in the storm, it's our job to go to the eye of the storm and P.A.U.S.E. so we are able to attend to their unmet needs. If our children could do that, they would. The same is true with everyone else. We are doing the work, so let's take charge.

Another well-known tool to release one-sided perspectives and realistically assess one's mental and emotional states is H.A.L.T:

- Hungry
- Angry
- Lonely
- Tired.

To recap, we now know that our job as conscious individuals is to shift our focus from people's misbehavior to underlying reasons behind the behavior. Our job is to see the problem areas as opportunities to heal our own inner child and create more meaningful connections with our loved ones. We learned that it's best to make an effort to purposefully increase acceptance, encouragement, connection, empathic mirroring, choices, playfulness, and humor, while decreasing expectation, criticism, fear, punishment, orders, control, and discontent when it comes to our interpersonal relationships. It sure is a colossal and challenging task, but I am certain you agree it's a noble one.

"For the faults of the many, judge not the whole.
Everything on earth is of mixed character, like a mingling of
sand and sugar. Be like the wise ant which seizes only the sugar,
and leaves the sand untouched."
—Mahavatar Babaji

Acceptance, encouragement, connection, choices, empathic mirroring, playfulness, humor

Expectation, criticism, fear, punishment, orders, control, abandonment, discontent

Notes for the Fourth Step of P.A.U.S.E.

Search for Different Perspectives

My takeaways:

_____

_____

_____

_____

_____

What do I commit to do **every day** to broaden my perspective and empower myself to take the fourth step of P.A.U.S.E. (Transcend the behavior, have an open mind, stop focusing on negative outlooks,...)?

_____

_____

_____

_____

_____

_____

CHAPTER SEVEN
FIFTH STEP OF P.A.U.S.E.: ELIMINATE FEAR AND PROCEED WITH LOVE AND COMPASSIONATE BOUNDARIES

The last step of P.A.U.S.E. is eliminating fear and proceeding with love and compassionate boundaries and win-win solutions. When we are at this stage, we have not only disengaged our defense mechanism, accepted the as-is, and felt our feelings, but we have also discovered the root causes of our triggers as well as the underlying reasons for people's behavior.

Why do we need to proceed with love and eliminate fear? Because "what's not love is a cry for love." As Dr. Martin Luther King Jr., the renowned American activist, said, "Darkness cannot drive out darkness; only light can do that. Hate cannot drive out hate; only love can do that."

We usually encounter people with the same energy as us during difficult times. If our partner is angry, we get angrier. If our children are frustrated, we get more frustrated. However, it's ideal to meet people with the antidote of their energy to balance out the dynamics in difficult situations. As an experiment, challenge yourself to be calm when people are agitated. Be compassionate when they are bitter. Be grounded when they are irritated. If your children are confused, encounter them with knowing energy. If your spouse lacks empathy, meet him with kindness.

Love vs. Fear Revisited Again

Love	Fear
Present	Past/Future
Formless - Heart	Form - Brain
Essence: Connection Conscious Awareness	Ego: Disconnection Past Memories
Conscious Choice	Compulsive Reaction
Abundance, Peace, Joy, Non-Judgmental Acceptance of As-Is, Discernment	Lack, Chronic Worry, Rage, Guilt, Shame, Apathy, Judgment
Growth / Creativity	Fight-Flight-Freeze / Survival
True	False

Our moment-by-moment realization that we either vibrate on fear or on love is the most potent catalyst for transformation. Think of these two states as two radio frequencies. When you select one, you inevitably pick the similar frequency from your surroundings unless you change the radio station.

Marianne Williamson, the American author, spiritual leader, and activist said, "Love is what we are born with. Fear is what we learn. The spiritual journey is the unlearning of fear and prejudices and the acceptance of love back in our hearts."

Our biological cells and our neurological wiring only have two states, *love* or *fear*. When we operate from love, our cells are in the growth mode. We vibrate high. We thrive. We heal. We feel love, joy, and peace. When we operate from fear, our cells are in survival mode. We don't grow or heal, and the majority of our mind-body system is shut down to be able to handle the perceived threat.

States of fear are essential at the time of real danger. Our body produces cortisol to take necessary and abrupt actions at these times. However, if we are chronically in the state of stress, fear, or anxiety, we fall ill because our cells have been deprived of a well-established growth mode.

These two states are the Yin and the Yang, the dark and the light. We don't judge them. We just become aware of their attributes and get to know them on a deeper level so we can quickly shift our attention from survival to growth, fear to love, scarcity to abundance, and suffering to joy.

Our inner compass is built on our feelings. Things that feel good in our heart and are aligned with our values usually vibrate on love. Rollo May, who is known as the father of existential psychotherapy, said, "Our feelings guide us, like the rudder of a ship." We are happier and our bodies are healthier when we operate in love.

Fully engaging in the present-moment experiences, such as walking, eating, and doing daily tasks literally exhausts the limited resources of our working memory. This prevents our brain from ruminating and regretting the past or worrying about the future. This is why the present moment is under the love column, whereas the past and future are on the fear side.

Our egoic mind naïvely believes we are doing something by worrying about the future or wallowing in the past. That is why we need to reclaim our power from our three, four or five-year-old brain and change the frequency of our vibration.

You might say, "But sometimes our fears are legitimate." What I mean by fear is the constant and unconscious nagging of our fear-based and anxious thoughts. If your worry is inspiring you to take healthy action, pay attention to it. However, when nothing can be done to change the current situation, use your mindfulness muscle to shift the frequency to that of abundance, peace, joy, and the non-judgmental acceptance of the as-is.

Give yourself permission to attend to the low-vibration feelings as you feel them to heal them. Then tune into higher frequencies. Sometimes, even the awareness of those feelings can abruptly shift the vibration. The trick is to go through the previous steps of P.A.U.S.E. to dismantle the fight-flight-freeze system that feeds off past memories and future-oriented fear-based thoughts.

Know that healing light and infinite love reside in your heart, while the ego dwells in your lower brain as a series of neural pathways that were formed mainly from the age of zero to seven. The heart is in the present moment and is aligned with our true nature.

Most fears are lies, delusions, and illusions. They are merely stories in our brain and aren't real. They are a waste of resources and the cause for our physical and emotional diseases and premature aging.

Use the following worksheet to empower yourself not only to see the silver lining in each adversity but the invaluable treasure hidden within its core. Let's get alchemizing!

Time to Alchemize

Adverse Life Condition / Adverse Thought	Hidden Treasure or Lesson / Flipped or Empowering Thought

One of the most effective ways to raise our vibration to love is to foster awareness of our unconscious thoughts and release the three henchmen of fear, control, and expectation.

Any futuristic anxiety, fear of judgment, our need to control, resisting the as-is, and expecting the current situation to be different are causes of suffering. Any of these have the ability to rob us from the richness of the present moment as well as our own impeccable wholeness and luminous divinity. I use three mantras for each of these phenomena:

- *Fear:* All is good at all times.
- *Control:* Control is an illusion.
- *Expectation:* I cannot expect a cat to bark.

Knowing that love and fear are the only two distinct states that we operate from, we can make it a practice to tune back to love when we detect chronic fear-based thinking. In order to make this switch, we might first be able to cultivate cognizance of our thoughts as shown in the first step of P.A.U.S.E. and then question them.

Eliminating fear and moving forward with love is the only conscious way to live life with joy, ease, grace, and flow as we create long-lasting and meaningful connections within ourselves and others. We can't coerce others to behave better by making them feel worse. When people feel better, they do better. If we act out of fear, we're probably reacting in such a way that creates shame in people as well as in ourselves, and the vicious cycle continues.

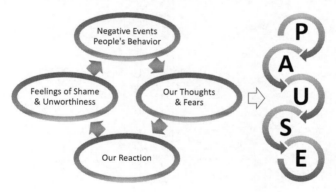

We now have two choices. One is the *what-if* route. This is when we unconsciously sulk and whine for not having a fantasy child, a prince charming, the "right" partner, or more zeros on our bank account balance. We throw tantrums and let our ego or fear-based programs take over. We resort to fixing situations in haste and anxiety, project our desires and fears onto people around us, and unknowingly create shame and deeper chasms between us and within us.

The other choice is to take the *what-is* route where we P.A.U.S.E. and proceed with love for oneself and others. This is when we don't resent, resist, or judge because we know adverse experiences are stepping stones to deeper self-realization and greater self-fulfillment.

Pema Chödrön, the Buddhist teacher and author, suggests, "Nothing ever goes away until it has taught us what we need to know." We constantly take on a curious mind to catapult us forward in our personal growth, releasing suffering and victimhood. Here is a review of P.A.U.S.E.

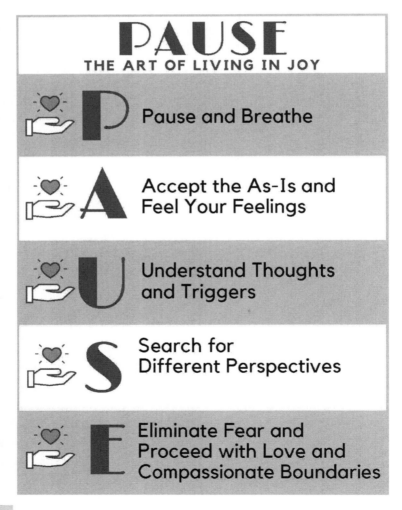

PAUSE
THE ART OF LIVING IN JOY

P Pause and Breathe

A Accept the As-Is and Feel Your Feelings

U Understand Thoughts and Triggers

S Search for Different Perspectives

E Eliminate Fear and Proceed with Love and Compassionate Boundaries

Connection Before Correction

As Dr. Shefali suggests, conscious relationships require two wings, connection and containment or boundaries. If we reinforce boundaries with people without making a connection with them, we create power struggles and deepen our disconnection with them.

People do not like us for us; they like us because of the way we make them feel about themselves. All humans like to be seen, accepted, and unconditionally loved. Although behaviors sometimes superficially mismatch this inner incentive, the truth remains unchanged. Love blooms in freedom and unshackling of all dependencies, and consequently we release expectations and resentment, helping love prevail.

I'll go over some tools to help you connect to people and make them feel seen, free, loved, valued, and accepted. Who knows, the conflict may dissolve by taking these steps, and we might not even have to set any boundaries. Here are some practices to foster connection.

- Follow the 80-20 rule. Make your words and behavior feel good to people at least 80% of the time.
- Release control because it creates disconnection.
- Play with your loved ones as much as you can. Playing is children's language, and we all have inner children who yearn to play.
- Be fully present with your loved ones when you are in their vicinity. Make them feel seen, heard, loved, and accepted. Put away your electronics.
- Use encouraging words with your loved ones.
- Use empathic mirroring when people are in distress or in a conflict with you.
- Spend at least ten minutes with undivided attention with the people in your close circle every day.
- As you gaze into their eyes, shower your loved ones with a few moments of love, acceptance, and gratitude. Kiss them with your eyes!

- Give 20-second hugs to your loved ones after long separation periods. Remember that hugs help our body produce oxytocin. Virginia Satir, the author and therapist, said, "We need four hugs a day for survival. We need eight hugs a day for maintenance. We need twelve hugs a day for growth."

Boundaries

"Boundaries are the distance at which
I can love you and me simultaneously"
– Prentis Hemphill

Only when we have paused, felt our feelings, inquired about the causes of our triggers, been curious about other perspectives, and connected with people on a deeper level are we ready to reinforce boundaries.

We usually assume that boundaries are about other people, whereas we need to set boundaries within ourselves. No matter how much we take care of ourselves, meditate, eat well, and exercise, if we aren't okay with saying *no*, our self-care bucket will always leak. This will leave us constantly feeling depleted and on edge. The extent we are firm with our boundaries on the outside is the extent we care about our wellbeing and peace of mind. If we are wishy-washy with our no's, people will shove and push until they get their way.

If your feelings are about to escalate to rage and helplessness, honor yourself and your boundaries in the moment and excuse yourself for a breather. Almost everything can wait. Real life-or-death situations are truly rare.

Rise above your ego defense mechanism that unrealistically overdramatizes life. That is its job, not yours. Your job as a fully grown adult is to take charge of your wellbeing and reclaim your power from the ego. Ego fights to be right. Leave the conflict either physically or emotionally. This way you not only tame your ego, you show others how much you honor yourself and your boundaries.

Usually we co-create our circumstances by subconsciously attempting to preserve our image of being the "good" person, not knowing we are doing a disservice to ourselves and others. When we say no when we want to say yes or say yes when we want to say no, we deplete our life force, build up resentment and expectation, and consequently damage our relationship with others. Be firm in setting compassionate boundaries. They aren't selfish; they are necessary.

When it comes to healthy boundaries, Eckhart Tolle brilliantly recommends picking one of three options. "When you complain, you make yourself a victim:

- Leave the situation,
- Change the situation
- Or accept it.

All else is madness."

Not being cognizant of our energetic capacity will not only exhaust us, it will aggravate matters in almost all situations. If we want to maintain our agency, sovereignty, and sanity, we must choose one of these three options. Otherwise we perpetually destine ourselves to be the victims and sufferers.

When it comes to children, Dr. Shefali introduces two kinds of rules—negotiable and non-negotiable. Non-negotiable rules are life-affirming and must not exceed a few, such as fastening seatbelts, brushing teeth, and other wellbeing matters. Logical consequences for these rules need to be assigned respectfully and in advance at a family meeting. For example, "We can go to the park when you wear your helmet."

The best way to learn for children is through experiences. Use school, weather, and bodily sensations for your advantage. Forgetting homework one day and having to go through the natural consequences in school will be way more effective than reminding them numerous times every day.

It's essential to articulate rules without attaching emotions, speaking:

- Clearly
- Calmly
- Completely

Otherwise you experience a power struggle. After all the rules were assigned by the whole family, so it isn't you who is imposing a consequence. The child has known the consequences and has decided to make their choice anyway. This will restore their autonomy. Have a few non-negotiable rules and go for a win-win negotiation for the rest.

Unfortunately, the one and only tool to gain cooperation or correct behavior in traditional parenting is through bribing or punishing, such as taking away privileges or giving time-outs. In conscious parenting, we make sure we have invested enough in-our children's bank account by filling up their connectedness, competence, and autonomy buckets on a daily basis.

Asking for cooperation, especially if it isn't attractive to the kids, resembles withdrawing from their accounts. We will experience power struggles and pushbacks if their accounts are empty or half-full. We must first employ our primary tools from our tool belt, such as connection, emotional coaching, curiosity, validation, play, and humor to gain cooperation and mitigate conflicts. The reinforcement of consequences must be the last resort and only 10% of the time. The bottom line is that if we want our children to do something without power struggles, we need to create the conditions, so they want to do it. This can be done by associating good memories with the task.

When it comes to our partners, keep in mind that they are not here to fulfill all our needs or even make us happy. Only we are responsible to make ourselves happy. Having this approach will always prevent us from going to the victim position.

Expecting another to genuinely know our innermost needs and be able to fulfill them is basically futile. They simply cannot do this. It's our job to perpetually deepen our understanding of ourselves and our needs so we can learn to meet them. This way, we come to a relationship whole and complete. We respect our own boundaries, and we allocate time and energy to our own self-care.

After our cup is full, we might want a few bonus items from our partner. This is the time we communicate our boundaries with them from a place of wholeness and needlessness, letting them know what we want from them. If I ask you, "My dear, it will really help me if you would do so and so for me. I would truly appreciate it," would you not want to help me out? Everyone wants to feel helpful and needed. It is just a matter of communicating our needs in such a way that the person wants to help and feel competent. The problem is that we usually start communicating our needs with a criticism. This will immediately place the person in a defen-sive position and block all communication.

Next time you need to communicate your boundaries or needs to people:

- First, validate their feelings, pains, struggles, and perspect-ives.
- Then communicate your boundary with calmness, clarity, and compassion.
- Remember you're the one who needs to honor your boun-daries, not others.

Family Meetings

Frustrations and family rules can be communicated in a family meeting. Here are some guidelines for family meetings:

- Have them on a specific day like Sunday.
- Have them short and sweet, especially if you have young children.
- Use a talking stick. Whoever holds it is the speaker.
- Start by saying something nice about your week.
- Then everyone gets a chance to talk about their frustration from the week.
- Everyone in the circle comes up with a solution.
- To end, everyone shares something they are grateful for. Everyone must follow this formula when they communi-cate their frustrations:"I feel... (fill in the blank) when ... (fill in the blank)."

Take your children's solutions seriously. Usually, they come up with brilliant ideas. They work because they are their solutions. I remember the time I was chronically frustrated about my kids getting ready in the mornings a few years back.

In a family meeting, I said, "I feel frustrated that I have to ask you guys many times to get out of bed, eat your breakfast, and dress up in the morning." My son's solution was to put water on his face. And you know what? I did, and it worked!

Practice Self Compassion

It's essential to set boundaries such that you can take care of yourself first. Think of the oxygen mask that needs to be put on yourself first. Remember that you want to give from the over-flow of your energy to others. Since you cannot pour from an empty cup, fill your cup first and make sure it isn't leaking.

To prevent leaking:

- Accept yourself, warts and all.
- Drop guilt and shame.
- Choose inner peace over being right.
- Release fear, control, expectation.
- Have firm boundaries.
- Learn to say *no.*

Use the space at the end of this section to write a list of what fills your cup. Here are some examples:

- As soon as you wake up in the morning, remember at least three things you have in life and cultivate gratitude for them. Keep the feeling for at least 20 seconds.
- Meditate daily for at least 10 minutes.
- Spend time in nature regularly.
- Eat wholesome foods.
- Sleep between 7 to 9 hours, and meditate before sleep.
- Listen to music and chant.
- Exercise daily for at least 15 minutes.
- Invest in your personal development.
- Create something every day.

- Spend quality time with each of your family members every day.

- Spend quality time with your friends and other loved ones regularly.

- Every time you see yourself in the mirror, say, "I love you."

- Set hourly reminders for yourself to acknowledge what you have accomplished that day. For example, you showered your child with love in the morning, you greeted your partner with affection, you meditated, you did your daily exercise, you successfully finished your work task, you cooked a healthy meal, you cleaned the house, you reached out to friends or family members to see how they were doing, you were kind to your neighbor.

- Keep affirming to yourself, "I'm enough. I'm lovable. I'm worthy. I'm abundant. I deserve to live in joy. I deserve to have it all. I choose peace." Our mind believes what we say to it.

If you're like me and your analytical mind needs some science, know that our body can naturally produce happiness chemicals when we commit to this list. Our body has an internal intelligent healing mechanism. For example, when we cut our fingers, our body quickly conjures up processes that automatically get down to the healing business—this is the work of our inner physician. When we feel sad, we cry, which helps to release oxytocin and endorphins to make us feel calm and ease the pain—this is the work of our inner psychologist.

Knowing we have an inner healer, we can take advantage of these mechanisms to preemptively raise our vibration to joy, love, and peace throughout the day. For example, we can intentionally help our body produce the feel-good hormones:

- *Endorphins:* we can exercise, laugh, and eat dark chocolate to help our body make endorphins to relieve pain, reduce stress, and improve our mood.

- *Dopamine:* We can listen to music, create, and learn something new to produce dopamine for pleasure and reward.

- *Serotonin*: To produce serotonin which is the cause of good mood, we can meditate, practice gratitude, and have a wholesome diet.

- *Oxytocin:* To create the love hormone or oxytocin, we can give and receive hugs, socialize, and do acts of kindness daily.

Healthy boundaries and being clear about our needs are imperative components of self-compassion. Write a list of your non-negotiable needs from your partner and use the conscious communication formula mentioned in chapter nine to communicate. You say, "What I need from you is..."

If you are stretched too thin between work and family and time is a precious commodity, taking one-minute breaks throughout the day can efficiently help to renew your self-care bucket. Use one-minute mindful breathing microbreaks to increase well-being, recovery from stress, and present-moment attention.

The Self-Care Iceberg

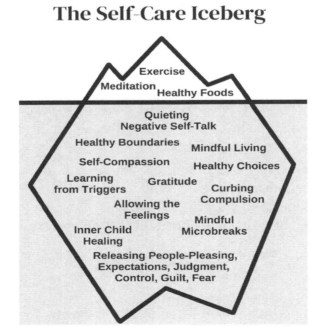

Your children need happy parents, your partner wants a happy companion, and so does everyone else. Caring about you first is caring about them. Recite, self-care is not selfish; it's necessary. Your main concern must be to P.A.U.S.E. and raise your vibration to joy, peace, love, and gratitude throughout the day as much as you can.

What-Brings-Me-Joy Exercise

Activities that help me cultivate joy, love, and peace individually:

On a daily basis:

_____

_____

Once a week:

_____

_____

Once a month:

_____

_____

Activities that help me cultivate joy, love, and peace with family members or friends:

On a daily basis:

_____

_____

Once a week:

_____

_____

Once a month:

_____

_____

"Neurons that fire together wire together." – Hebb's Law

According to Dr. Joe Dispenza, whose postgraduate education has been in neurology, neuroscience, and cellular biology, we use different parts of the brain as we acquire new knowledge, act on it, and then permanently embody it.

As we learn new knowledge, we use the *neocortex* or our thinking and intellectual brain. When we take the new knowledge, personalize it, and act on it and fire and wire new circuits, we use the *limbic* brain or the emotional or chemical brain. As we continually repeat the experience and don't have to consciously think about the process, we use the *cerebellum*. This is the time our body and our mind become one and the action becomes ingrained in our subconscious.

As we increasingly choose different responses and rise above our ego defense mechanism by not criticizing our partner, not punishing our children, not texting or emailing unkind comments, and not meeting unkind people with similar attitude, we fire and wire new ways of living. When we install the new circuitry in our brain, our wise and compassionate way of living replaces the old ones. The neurological reason for successful brain reprogramming is that we have a finite amount of neural growth factor that acts as *glue* in the neural networks of our brain.

Imagine that network A is our pattern of yelling or abandoning when we feel helpless and triggered and network B is our new way of taking a P.A.U.S.E. As we replace our old way with the new way, network B has no choice but to borrow some glue off network A since there is a limited amount of neural growth factor in our brain. The more we fire the neurons in network B, the more glue we need to take away from network A. There will be a time that network A gets entirely depleted of neural growth factor, and tears up. This causes network B to be the only dominant response pattern and we no longer yell or abandon in the face of a conflict.

It took several months for Dr. Dispenza to overcome his doubt and fear, healing his spine with only his mind after a terrible car accident. He was advised to undergo a radical surgery after a car hit him during his bicycle ride in a triathlon or he would probably never walk again. He decided to reconstruct his entire shattered spine vertebrae by vertebrae by only using the power of his mind, and he did so in three months. He believed that "the power that made the body, heals the body" and demonstrated the legitimacy of this belief to the whole world by not giving into his ANTs.

Every time I feel disappointed that I have relapsed into old ways of reactivity and powerlessness, I remember how Dr. Dispenza's perseverance manipulated matter over time. We can all agree that manipulating the mind must be much easier. By not focusing on perfection and accepting our human journey of falling and rising up, we traverse the path from fear to love with ease, grace, and joy without being harsh and judgmental with ourselves.

Two renowned addiction researchers, Carlo Di Clemente and James O. Prochaska came up with a six-stage model of change that promotes encouragement in the personal development journey and helps to put the rational mind at ease at the inevitable times of relapse in the recovery process. Keep in mind that addiction does not end with only substance abuse. It can entail many mental or behavioral habits and patterns, such as frequent rage, depression, chronic anxiety, perfectionism, overeating, impulsive shopping, and over-pleasing.

In this model, the first stage is the *precontemplation* phase where the person has no intention of changing behavior. The next stage is *contemplation*. This is when a person is aware a problem exists but has no commitment to action. This is usually the stage a husband is in when the wife has coerced him to come to me in hopes of better communication. Next is *preparation* when a person is intending to take an action. *Action* or the active modification of behavior is the next step. This is where the limbic brain gets involved. Sustained change is the *maintenance* phase, and the last and sixth stage is *relapse.* This is when we fall back to the old patterns of behavior.

Nevertheless, there is a catch here. Relapsing doesn't mean regression. Depending on our outlook, this is the time an adversity can become a steppingstone to propel us to a higher plane. This is why this model is an upward spiral. We learn from our relapses and grow stronger, wiser, and more resilient. This is where our life gets as good as our mindset.

Stages of Change

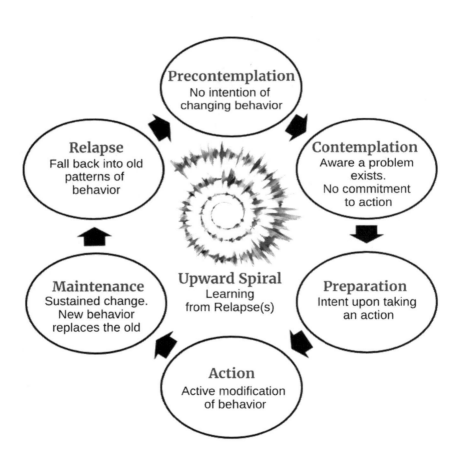

We can either give into our perfectionistic propensities and feel guilty for our shortcomings or accept our humanness. We can remember we are love-programming the brain that is 95%

programmed for fear during childhood. We can remind ourselves that we must first love ourselves, warts and all, if we expect others to love us. We must first see ourselves as worthy if we want to create a worthy life.

An effective brain reprogramming exercise to rewire our brain from fear to love and from limitation to abundance is to intentionally replace our sabotaging ANTs by more empowering beliefs. Please use this space to firstly shed light on your limiting beliefs and thoughts that were mainly formed in childhood during the first seven years. Secondly come up with positive affirmations you can use on a daily, even hourly basis to rewire your brain for more joy, peace, abundance, and freedom.

Be watchful of the bully in your mind that ceaselessly disparages you and finds faults with what you do and who you are. Be aware that the incessant voice in your mind is barely an encourager and always a scolder, a nagger, and a blamer because it was formed in childhood. We must admit that we are regurgitating the blaming voice of our parents when we could not possibly live up to their unrealistic expectations of us.

It's now time to take charge and perpetually re-parent ourselves through self-encouragement, loving ourselves unconditionally and believing that we are enough just the way we are. We must keep reminding the little child in us that we matter, and we don't have to do anything, have anything, or be anyone to earn the love we inherently deserve.

Besides repeating your affirmations during mediation, please say them out loud every morning while looking at yourself in the mirror and standing with a power pose. As previously stated, this way we take advantage of the influences of our body on our mind. Research shows standing firm and powerful similar to the superman's pose instills confidence and resilience in the mind, the same way smiling and laughing influences the mind to be happy.

Daily Brain Reprogramming Exercise

How do I bully myself? ANTs (Automatic Negative Thoughts)	How can I affirm myself? Daily Positive Affirmations

As you're transforming into a more actualized version of yourself, release comparison. It's the killer of joy. If you want to compare anything, compare yourself to the day before. Even one instance of not giving into despair, rage, fear, and anxiety is a moment for celebration.

Invest *daily* in your self-care and self-empowerment to fire the neurons you intend to fire, not the ones you are predisposed to. Have science-based faith that "neurons that fire together finally wire together." Zig Ziglar, an American author and motivational speaker said, "People often say that motivation does not last. Well, neither does bathing; that's why we recommend it daily."

"Every time you are tempted to react in the same old way, ask if you want to be a prisoner of the past or a pioneer of the future." —Deepak Chopra

Notes for the Fifth Step of P.A.U.S.E.

Eliminate Fear and Proceed with Love and Compassionate Boundaries

My takeaways:

_____

_____

_____

_____

_____

_____

What do I commit to do **every day** to proceed with love and empower myself to take the fifth step of P.A.U.S.E. (Self-care, boundaries, choose love over fear,...)?

_____

_____

_____

_____

_____

_____

CHAPTER EIGHT
CONSCIOUS PARENTING

According to Dr. Shefali, the founder of conscious parenting, "A conscious parent is not one who seeks to fix her child or seek to produce or create the 'perfect' child. The parent understands that this child has been called forth to 'raise the parent' itself."

Traditionally, we fallaciously believe our children are ours and we have all the right to manipulate them, coerce them, and mold them to fit our fantasies and our own unfulfilled desires. This is far from the truth.

The bitter truth is that we decide to have children for our own self-serving reasons. As we erroneously assume academic degrees, secure jobs, spouses, and houses must fill our inner hole and appease our broken heart, bearing children is mainly the next item on the list. Of course, the phenomenon of social conformity doesn't help either. Kahlil Gibran, poet and philosopher, exquisitely portrayed the true parent-child relationship in his book *The Prophet:*

"Your children are not your children.
They are the sons and daughters of Life's longing for itself.
They come through you but not from you,
And though they are with you yet they belong not to you.
You may give them your love but not your thoughts,
For they have their own thoughts.
You may house their bodies but not their souls,
For their souls dwell in the house of tomorrow,

> which you cannot visit, not even in your dreams.
> You may strive to be like them,
> but seek not to make them like you.
> For life goes not backward nor tarries with yesterday.
> You are the bows from which
> your children as living arrows are sent forth.
> The archer sees the mark upon the path of the infinite,
> and He bends you with His might
> that His arrows may go swift and far.
> Let your bending in the archer's hand be for gladness;
> For even as He loves the arrow that flies,
> so He loves also the bow that is stable."
> —Kahil Gibran

Unlike typical styles of parenting, conscious parenting has lit-tle to do with children and a lot to do with parents. Similar to everyone and every event in our life, our children pinpoint with the highest precision where we must heal and grow.

Our children can be our greatest awakeners and teachers if we allow it. If you are a parent, I'm sure you agree that you are most susceptible to being triggered by your children than anyone, especially after and around when they turn two or into teenagers. This means you have called them to your life to help you evolve further.

"Because-I-said-so," or traditional parenting, being a top- down model uses the power of authority and employs punitive measures, either physical and/or mental, to coerce children to do what parents want. What do you think we teach in this parenting style? Are we not showing that bigger or older has more authority? Are we not promoting dictatorship?

The popular style of parenting that is based on behavioristic principles is equally manipulative. It uses rewards, either tangible or intangible, and punishments such as timeouts, grounding, and taking away privileges. What do we teach in this style? Are we not promoting extrinsic motivators, such as fear and bribes?

If these are our only tools, how can children learn to do the "right" thing intrinsically without a fear of punishment or a hope for a reward? How could they strengthen their muscles of autonomy, independent thinking, and a moral compass?

While the mainstream parenting as well as our school system have been adopting this style for the past decades, it's essential to know that the main experimental subjects for the science of behaviorism were animals—dogs, pigeons, and rats. I am sure we all agree that humans deserve to be looked at more holistically than other sentient beings.

Conscious parenting, unlike the other two styles, transcends the child's behavior and attends to the underlying root causes of behavior as we discussed in the fourth step of P.A.U.S.E. It also views the child equal in value and essence as the parent and as a purposeful and sovereign throbbing spirit in the cosmos. This style uses and teaches respect, democracy, connection, cooperation, empathy, discernment, love and compassion, problem-solving, authentic living, and the law of cause and effect.

At the root of traditional and behavioristic parenting is fear. Besides instilling fear in children to falsely fabricate extrinsic motivation through fear of authority or fear of punishment, the parents are also eternally in fear themselves. Are we not almost always in fear of losing control and not fulfilling our personal, societal, and familial expectations and fantasies, such as raising well-behaved children, straight-A students, high-achieving athletes, successful future employees, and eventually happily married adults with a handful of grandchildren?

When we experience fear, we unconsciously make all the efforts to take control of every situation. In almost all situations, taking control of someone creates disconnection.

Dr. Siegel demonstrated the ineffectiveness of the first two styles of parenting when he said, "Too often we forget that discipline really means to teach, not to punish. A disciple is a student, not a recipient of behavioral consequences."

We forget this because we are hurt ourselves, and unless we heal our wounded inner child, we will not be able to parent our real child consciously, wisely, and compassionately. Only when we have taken sufficient P.A.U.S.E. are we able to create conditions for our children to blossom into their authentic self without us constantly projecting our fears and our desires onto them. We become their keen ushers rather than authoritarian figures.

Conscious parenting crafts a deeper meaning for raising children. It allows us not to get trapped in power struggles of tooth-brushing and homework. It helps us understand our children are not ours to mold but alchemic agents for our change and transformation. They are our best mindfulness teachers. Have you noticed how they throw a tantrum in one minute and laugh in the next? They live their present-moment experiences unapologetically and fiercely. They only live to play. We, on the other hand, eat to work and work to eat. We don't truly live or play!

Every time we get triggered by our children or feel confused, overwhelmed, or helpless, we receive a new opportunity to look within, P.A.U.S.E., and evolve to a higher plain in the spiral of our evolution. "To zone in on the parent-child dynamic is to heal the planet," says Dr. Shefali.

> *"There is no single effort more radical in its potential for*
> *saving the world than a transformation*
> *of the way we raise our children."*
> —*Marianne Williamson*

CHAPTER NINE
CONSCIOUS RELATIONSHIPS

Similar to every other undertaking in our life, we strive to find happiness in a partner. My best advice to those who are at the verge of diving into a relationship is to P.A.U.S.E. and memorize and internalize the roadmap to unconditional joy and inner peace first. This will ensure you will attract a person with the same frequency of abundance, love, and joy so you will not go on a hamster wheel of chasing one another to fulfill your needs.

Once you learn to build your life with intention and are not influenced by familial, cultural, and societal shackles, the "right" person will emerge to take you to even higher grounds of consciousness with ease and grace. This pause is especially necessary if we have already experienced a relationship that hasn't worked, otherwise we repeat the same pattern in future relations.

Our life patterns start in childhood. If we had an alcoholic parent, there is a high chance we will marry one. If we had a controlling parent, there is a high chance we will marry one too. To uncover these childhood wounds and heal them is essential, or else we regurgitate the patterns. The bottom line is if we don't P.A.U.S.E. to scrutinize our inner psyche and attend to our inner needs, we chase our tail.

When couples come to me, I make sure they understand that our time together will first and foremost revolve around the solo journey of learning the *Art of Living in Joy*. Each of them is supposed to embody the teachings independent of each other. This means, no more blaming, begrudging, criticizing, and finger-pointing, since no one is responsible to make anyone happy.

Once this is done diligently, wisely, and responsibly, the by- product will be a happy partnership. This is the foundation of conscious couple work. The communication tools and tech-niques will just be the icing on the cake.

When Relationships Fail

It's essential to switch our criteria of a "good" marriage or partnership from longevity to growth. Suppose our relationship is void of personal and relational growth and filled with emotional battles and destructive habits, but we are unwilling to do the inner work. In that case, there is a significant chance that the relationship will end.

Dr. John Gottman, an American psychologist who has worked for over four decades on divorce prediction and marital stability, predicted with over 90% accuracy that relationships fail with the presence of four negative communication patterns:

1. Criticism or verbally attacking someone's character. The antidote is to talk about your feelings and needs and make gentle requests using "I" statements.

2. Contempt or insulting. The antidote is remembering and being grateful for the other person's positive attributes.

3. Defensiveness and reversing blame. The antidote is seeing the other person's perspectives, accepting responsibility, and apologizing for your wrongdoing.

4. Stonewalling or avoiding. The antidote is taking a break, practicing self-soothing, doing some self-care, and getting back to conscious communication.

It's pivotal to perpetually make an effort to see other people's viewpoints by fully embodying their positions and feeling their pains and struggles. I usually ask my clients to dissolve themselves for a moment to see if they can experience the world from their partners' perspectives. That's why similar to conscious parenting, validating and empathizing is always a surefire way to put out the fire between couples and cultivate more connection, understanding, and intimacy.

Conscious Communication

One great tool that empowers conscious couples to be strong teammates is understanding each other's love language. Dr. Gary Chapman, the author of *The Five Love Languages* series, has some online quizzes you can download to uncover the love languages you, your partner, and even your children communicate with. At the beginning of our marriage, I remember my husband would offer me a glass of water without me asking for it. Later, I found out this was his way of expressing his love to me. He assumed my love language was *acts of service* just like him.

On the other hand, when I discovered *physical touch* was my love language, not his, I emancipated both of us from expecting him to meet my needs. Every time, I wanted to be hugged, I would go to him and hug him. It did not matter to me who initiated the hug. It was the hug I was aiming for—and rest assured, I got it.

This way, I got my rush of oxytocin, evaded building up expectation and resentment, and avoided unnecessary conflicts I had initially endured in our relationship. When I look back, I see how unreasonable it was to expect each other to fill each other's love cup without knowing what our love languages were. I had no idea what mine was, let alone his. Expecting a cat to bark comes to mind once again.

We all adopt our love languages through childhood programming. This is part of the reason I tell my couple clients not to communicate with each other directly at the first session. I do feel one speaks Italian and the other Japanese. They certainly need an interpreter before they could suc-cessfully learn each other's languages, otherwise all will be lost in translation. The love languages include *receiving gifts, quality time, words of affirmation, acts of service, and physical touch.*

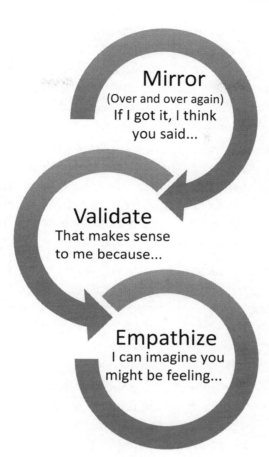

When it comes to conscious communication and active listening, I recommend the work of Dr. Harville Hendrix and Dr. Helen La-Kelly Hunt. The world would be a better place if we communicated our feelings instead of criticizing the other person, and if we listened with empathy instead of defending ourselves. The fabulous model that Dr. Hendrix and Dr. Hunt developed is an extraordinary catalyst in making this happen. The following paragraphs are my adaptation of their work.[23]

---

23   *Getting the Love You Want* by Dr. Harville Hendrix and Dr. Helen LaKelly Hunt

This tool can be used in various settings such as parenting, couple relationships, friendship, sibling relationships, schools, at work, and even governments. When we listen to people, we listen to respond, not to listen. When we have a difference of opinions, we do it through criticism, which shuts down all channels for communication. If we want to increase relational harmony and world peace, we need a new way of communicating.

We must dismantle the fight-flight-freeze system and speak and listen *intentionally* if we want to do this the right way. A very rigid formula needs to be followed by the speaker and the listener to make this protocol work. At first, following the rules might feel awkward, but after experiencing the brilliance of this method, you will lean into adopting it.

The rule for the speaker is to speak in short sentences and start the sentences with *I*, preferably with the structure, *I feel...when....* Last but not least, there cannot be *criticism*. It's essential that the speaker does some self-discovery (the third step of P.A.U.S.E.) and tries to understand which childhood memory might have triggered the feeling in the current situation.

For example, this was the conversation I had with my husband before we finally resolved his abandonment strategy at the time of conflict: "I feel judged when you stop talking to me after we have a conflict about the kids. I feel you judge me as a parent. I remember I felt judged and watched over all the time as a kid because I was expected to be the best at all times." This self-reflection not only brought me cathartic healing, it certainly was an epiphany for my husband to the point his pattern of *flight* entirely vanished.

Here is a guideline for the listener:

1. *Mirror* : "If I got it right, I think you said..."

2. *Validate*: "That makes sense to me because..."

3. *Empathize*: "I can imagine you might be feeling..."

For the last two steps, make yourself vanish temporarily and try to truly put yourself in their shoes to see their perspective and feel their pain. This does not mean you are condoning their wrongdoing or agreeing with what they say. It just means you are validating their point of view and empathizing with their feelings.

No one can forbid anyone to feel a certain way. All feelings are legitimate. As far as perceptions are concerned, it's futile to expect others to have the same worldview as us as we discussed in the fourth step of P.A.U.S.E. Do you remember the shadows of the cylinder on the perpendicular walls or Rumi's Elephant in the Dark parable?

After going through the protocol, articulate your need this way: "It would really help me if..." or, "What I need from you is..."

At the end of this section, it is worth mentioning that molecular genetic study of humans argues that monogamy was untypical of human reproductive patterns until approximately 5,000 to 10,000 years ago. Nuclear families and monogamous relations appeared due to the emergence of sedentary farming communities in Europe and Asia, and then Africa and the Americas. We were created to live in communes with unwavering tribal support where we shared our food, our expertise, our families, and our duties. Although we might choose to live by this doctrine and have nuclear families, it's paramount that we don't lose awareness of our human nature and have compassion and respect for each other and our children.

It's crucial to know what love is. True love is needless, free of judgment, and fosters growth and freedom. Anything other than these is addiction and dependency. If we want to have thriving relationships, we should never lose sight of this profound but hard truth.

CHAPTER TEN
CLAIMING THE SACRED GIFT

The Cave of the Heart

"The heart is the hub of all sacred places. Go there, and roam."
—Bhagawan Nityananda

It's imperative that we don't overlook the wisdom of our heart or our intuition. There is a difference between knowledge and wisdom. We usually acquire a piece of knowledge from the outside and house it in our brain. Wisdom, however, resides within our heart either because of an inner experience or an unwavering sense of knowing.

Rumi said, "Everything in the universe is within you. Ask all from yourself." This is not just some esoteric concept, but a scientific fact. Through rigorous objective experimentation, researchers have found that our heart knows what our eyes have not yet perceived.

Albert Einstein said something aligned with Rumi's quote: "The intuitive mind is a sacred gift, and the rational mind is a faithful servant. We have created a society that honors the servant and has forgotten the gift."

The trick is to allow our heart to lead while letting the rational mind support the inspiration. Science shows that the heart is not just a muscle. It's an intelligent energy center. Unless we learn to decipher its language, our knowledge is incomplete. We can always use our logic, but we must know that it's limited. It's pivotal to be open to our intuition and inner guidance. Even Einstein trusted his intuition when it came to scientific theorization. It's said that he chose to sit in silence and look to the Alps for some time to intuitively know which alternative to select from a handful of possible solutions to the theory of relativity.

Intuition is the ability to obtain knowledge through an inner knowing or instinctively without rationalization or reasoning. If we have taken enough P.A.U.S.E.s, we are prepared and open to receive and perceive our inward answer. We just need to be willing to ask and be genuinely curious. "Ask and it is given!"

Having said this, it's vital to ask the right questions. If I ask why I'm struck with a series of bad luck, I might not only reinforce this thought and actualize the adverse vision, but the answer might not be of use for me at all. However, if I ask what lessons I need to receive from the unfavorable events or how I can better handle the situation with ease, grace, and joy, I can use the inspiration for realignment and personal evolution.

Rumi said, "Your task is not to seek for love, but merely to seek and find all the barriers within yourself that you have built against it." Taking a P.A.U.S.E. grants us the dominion and the permission to remove all the barriers within ourselves and revel in the cave of our heart where *all is well at all times*. In our heart, and between our thoughts, we are one with the cosmos and in full contact with our limitless intelligence. Ernest Holmes, an American New Thought teacher, said, "There is one power in the universe, and we can all use it."

Albert Einstein added, "We can't solve problems by using the same kind of thinking we used when we created them." Forming the habit of quieting the fear-thinking lets our intuitive abilities flourish and become increasingly accessible to us. Here are some of the tools through which we can strengthen this skill:

- Every morning, allow yourself to sit in silence for a few minutes. The goal is to quiet the mind. You can imagine you're taking an elevator from your brain to your heart or visualize you are switching off your analytical mind.
- Take deep breaths in and out of your heart to activate it.

- Put your hands on your heart, and curiously ask your Higher Self what your assignment is for the day.

- Ask your Higher Self to take over your tasks such that they get resolved with ease, gracefully, and joyfully. Make sure you surrender and fully trust.

- Every time a conflict arises, or you catch yourself in a negative state, P.A.U.S.E. and ask your Higher Self to inspire you with a course of action that contributes to your peace and that of humanity.

- Know that the aid of your inner guide is always within reach. Just make sure you ask good questions.

- Every time you want to make a hard decision, visualize each path and see how each one feels in your body. Pick the one that feels calm, expanded, consistent, and uplifting. You can make decisions ranging from what kind of food to eat to whether to purchase a house or not.

- You can learn and use applied kinesiology muscle testing tools to connect to and rely on your inner guidance for your decisions.[24]

The Binary Voices

Being aware that we have two distinct inner voices is elemental in knowing ourselves and retraining ourselves for more joy, peace, and love. One voice stems from our primitive and protective brain and our neurologically wired fear-based and self-criticizing thoughts and beliefs. This voice is distinctively loud and is present almost all the time.

The other voice rises from our inner knowing in our hearts and dwells between our thoughts. This voice is usually very low unless we intentionally turn its volume up and practice listening to it and honoring it. This is the sound of our inner wisdom, the one that rises like a phoenix from the ashes of fear and ignorance.

---

24   Kinesiology is a holistic and integrative methodology of natural health care that combines Eastern and Western knowledge to assess the body.

Our job as awakened humans is to lower the voice of fear-thinking and amplify the melodic sound of our hearts. Or we must at least use the protective voice of our limited mind in service of our higher mind or intuition, as Einstein suggested.[25]

We are born in a dualistic world to experience the spectrum of feelings, perceptions, and sensations. We could not have truly experienced pleasure if we had no understanding of pain, and we would not feel whole and at home if we never felt lost and scared.

Regardless of the existing polarity in the human world, through love we sometimes experience a unison with the cosmos and a sense of inner wholeness and bliss. It almost seems we live in two different dimensions with completely different sets of rules, perceptions, and realities. It sometimes appears we are a whole other creature beneath the surface of human constraints and polarities. What if this assumption was actually true?

Each of our layers has exclusive capabilities. The loud voice that comes from our brain is bound to the physical plane, past information, our childhood acclimatization, and generational patterns. If and when we are awakened to the nature of this voice, rather than being blindly indoctrinated, we can use it like a "faithful servant" to serve the subtle voice or the sacred gift that germinates from our inner knowing and out of our connection with our Source.

This isn't possible unless we have befriended the inner roommate or the voice in our primitive brain and have become the master of our mind, our thoughts, and our stories. Knowing that this is the voice of our ego defense mechanism and was developed in our childhood to help us survive can give us an understanding of how to quiet it. A brilliant method to do this is to communicate with this voice.

Interestingly, this voice has two layers. The inner layer is the voice of the screaming inner child, and the outer shell is the voice

---

25   "The intuitive mind is a sacred gift, and the rational mind is a faithful servant. We have created a society that honors the servant and has forgotten the gift." – Albert Einstein

of the ego defense mechanism protecting the inner child. Next time you are caught in adverse feelings, P.A.U.S.E. and communicate with your ego and say, "Thank you for trying to protect me, but I don't need your services now."

Next, communicate with your inner child. Bring her into your heart and say, "I'm sorry you're going through this. You don't deserve it. I'm so sorry you feel alone and scared. I've got you now. You don't have to worry anymore. You're safe. You're loved. You're enough. You're free. Just go play. I've got this."

Similar to the voice in your head, in order to raise the volume of the voice in your heart, you must communicate with it. The best way to converse with the inner voice is to communicate through good questions. Asking questions is an art by itself. Take a couple of deep breaths into your heart to activate it, and then ask questions such as:

"How can I approach this situation with ease, grace, and joy?"

"What response is aligned with my Higher Self?"

"What should I say and how should I say it to cultivate more love and peace?"

"What's needed now?"

You can also seek solace and assistance of your Higher Self before embarking on a task or when you are going through challenges. Before my talks, classes, and private sessions, I close my eyes, take a deep breath, put my hand on my heart, and say, "Let the words I articulate to my clients or students alleviate their pain and elevate their consciousness, my own consciousness, and humanity's as a whole."

Let the words or the answers come effortlessly. They usually don't take more than five seconds to rise. The more you practice surrendering and listening, the more you notice the quality of the voice from your heart is worlds apart from that of your protective brain. One feels contracted and unsafe, the other expansive and soothing. Trust and lean into the wisdom of your heart.

Meister Eckhart, a German philosopher, and mystic said, "There's a place in the soul where you've never been wounded." This is the place we tap into.

Expanding the Container

"You are not a drop in the ocean.
You are the entire ocean in a drop."
—Rumi

If we put a coin in a bucket of water, we can see the coin at the bottom. If we put the same coin in a shallow pool, we can still see the coin, although blurry. But if we put the same coin in the middle of the ocean, we are incapable of seeing it as it vanishes in the vastness of the ocean.

The coin is the analogy of a problem, whether physical, mental, or emotional. Sometimes simply enlarging the container and expanding our viewpoint can make the gravity of the problem diminish, dissolve, and even disappear. This involves altering our position from being trapped in the middle of the circle of miseries to an expansive aerial view from where we can observe the theater of our life free from judgment, expectation, and bias. Keep in mind that we practically need to expand our container on a moment-by-moment basis because our lower brain is always bombarding us with possible threats through *ANTs*.

Once we know all the people and events in our life are merely conduits for our growth and opportunities for our evolution, the only plausible and conscious reaction is our curiosity to know how we can heal and grow from such experiences. At any moment we have the choice to view ourselves as a victim of the circumstances or to escape Plato's Cave to find a more empowering perspective. It's always possible to interpret a circumstance to our advantage.

Everything involves a thought. We rejoice because of a thought, and we also suffer because of a thought. Considering thoughts are merely an effect of firing neurons in our brain, who has dominance over them? Doesn't our brain reside in our skull in our body? No one can inject, eliminate, or modify our thoughts without our permission.

Once we accept the ownership of our thoughts and feelings, we have expanded our container and know exactly how to handle what comes our way. This way it benefits us and liberates us instead of entrapping us further. Rather than wallowing in victim mentality, we can genuinely ask why our soul needed to call this experience into our lives.

As expressed in the Buddhist perspective, we may not be able to control the first arrow that life throws at us. However, we always have the choice to dodge the second arrow that's our own response to our experiences. The second arrow is always optional. It's the arrow we throw at ourselves based on our interpretation of the events in our life.

We expand our container through conscious awareness by untethering ourselves from our habits, repetitive behavior, and reactionary impulses. We can also liberate ourselves from our dependencies and preconceptions, and by releasing all expectations and resentment. Through living in the reality of the present and not a fantasy, we expand our container by choosing joy over and over again.

"You were born with wings, why prefer to crawl through life?"
—*Rumi*

Service is Joy

Tagore, the well-known poet and philosopher, said, "I slept and dreamt that life was joy. I awoke and saw that life was service. I acted and behold, service was joy."

Richard Barrett, a prolific author, developed a model of consciousness based on Maslow's hierarchy of human needs which places service to humanity and the planet at the seventh and most advanced level of consciousness. All seven levels from the lowest to highest are survival, relationship, self-esteem, transformation, self-expression, connection, and finally service that involves compassion and humility.

Observing the model closely, one can notice that the levels of consciousness are in accordance with the seven chakras or the energy points that reside in different parts of our spinal column. Studying chakras brings us much awareness about the interconnectedness of our physical, mental, and energetic bodies and can empower us greatly in our personal development journey.

Chakra in Sanskrit means "wheel" and refers to spinning vortexes of energy that influence our emotional and physical well-being. Each vortex is connected to the nerves, organs, and glands nearby. That is why pain and discomfort in our body can be a good indicator of an unbalanced or blocked chakra in that area and can help us view our physical and mental ailments holistically.

The root chakra, with the color red, is on the base of the spine and corresponds to physical senses, safety, and survival. Repeating the affirmation, "I am safe" is a powerful tool to bring balance to this energy vortex.

The sacral chakra, with the color orange, is below the naval and corresponds to feelings and relationships with the affirmation, "I am creative."

The solar plexus chakra, with the color yellow, is in the abdomen and corresponds to power and with the affirmation, "I am strong."

The heart chakra, with the color green, is in the center of the chest and corresponds to love and connection with the affirmation, "I am loved."

The throat chakra, with the color blue, is in the throat and coresponds to creativity and self-expression with the affirmation, "I am expressive."

The third eye chakra, with the color indigo, is in the middle of the eyebrows and corresponds to clear perception and intuition with the affirmation, "I am connected."

The crown chakra, with the color violet, is on the top of the head and corresponds to pure awareness with the affirmation, "I am divine."

Here is another set of affirmations to bring harmony and balance to chakras and their functions:

Root: I am.
Sacral: I feel.
Solar plexus: I do.
Heart: I love.
Throat: I speak.
Third eye: I see.
Crown: I understand.

The following chart contains the list of each chakra, signs of physical and emotional blockages, their related consciousness levels, and the affirmations we can use daily for bringing balance and realignment to our body, mind, and spirit. It's said that wearing, seeing, and visualizing chakra colors, and even eating the same-color food as a chakra, can help imbalanced chakras find their harmony. You can find more tips on the chart for unblocking and balancing chakras depending on your preference.[26]

26   Please note that this chart is a collection of data from various open sources. I was not able to credit this information properly as this knowledge first emerged in the early traditions of Hinduism four thousand years ago and has circulated endlessly on the World Wide Web. Furthermore, this data must not be used as a replacement for medical treatment or diagnosis.

Seven Chakras and Their Corresponding Consciousness Level

Chakra	Root	Sacral	Solar Plexus	Heart	Throat	Third Eye	Crown
Location	Base of the spine	Below the naval	Abdomen	Center of the chest	Throat	Between eyebrows	Top of the head
Color	Red	Orange	Yellow	Green	Blue	Indigo	Violet
Mantra Sound	LAM	VAM	RAM	YAM	HAM	KSHAM	OM
Principle and Tool of Recognition	Physical senses	Feelings	Power, will, personal understanding	Love, communal understanding	Creativity, universal understanding	Perception, imagination	Pure awareness
Glands	Adrenal	Gonad	Pancreas	Thymus	Thyroid	Pituitary	Pineal
Possible Sign of Physical Blockage	Constipation, fatigue	Painful periods, low sex drive, infertility	Poor digestion, low Blood sugar	Heart disease, high blood pressure	Thyroid problems, sore throat	Headaches, depression	Poor sleep habits
Harmonious	Easeful connection to all things physical	Balance and easy-going	Inner peace	Warm feelings of harmony and connection	Clear and calm speaker and listener	Clear sight, sixth sense	Spiritual tranquility
Disharmonious	Over-emphasis on all material things, unsafe, spacey, greed, egoism	Unable to express emotions, creative block, anxiety, pride	Low self-esteem, lack of willpower, suspicious about love	Lack of empathy, fear of intimacy, can't express feelings	Many words without clarity, can't express feelings	Fear, confusion, inflexibility, poor intuition	Restlessness, dissatisfaction, difficult to meditate, bodily disconnect
Consciousness Level	Survival	Relationships	Self-esteem	Transformation	Self-expression	Connection	Contribution
Description	Physical survival and safety	Harmonious relationships	Building sense of self-worth	Continuous growth and development	Finding meaning in existence	Making a difference in the community	Service to humanity and the planet
Stages of Development	Surviving	Conforming	Differentiating	Individuating	Self-actualizing	Integrating	Serving
Affirmation	I am	I feel	I do	I love	I speak	I see	I understand
Affirmation	I am safe	I am creative	I am strong	I am loved	I am expressive	I am connected	I am Divine

As we heal our past wounds, bring light to our shadows,[27] and cultivate compassion for ourselves and others, we traverse the consciousness levels and elevate our soul to higher awareness. As you see in the chakra chart, the heart chakra placed halfway in the chakra stack corresponds with the transformation level in the consciousness chart.

This is where most shifts happen in human consciousness. Since the heart energy center is the seat of transformation and integration, it acts as a bridge connecting our earthly and spiritual aspirations. It's crucial to be cognizant where our attention and energy go throughout the day. Do they lean more toward the three lower chakras below the heart chakra or the three above it?

Cultivating awareness of where we spend most of our time and energy is essential in creating transformation. The heart chakra is the focal point. If our heart energy is more inclined toward the lower three chakras, we may foster egoism, greed (root), jealousy (sacral), and pride (solar plexus). However, if our heart is more engaged in the upper chakras, we cultivate more compassion and move toward elation and wholeness.

As we traverse and sustain the chakras, we evolve in our healing journey. It's essential to work on one's materialistic and physical health and safety first (root) to be able to have a thriving relationship with others (sacral). Similarly, we must feel balanced and be able to have open communication with others (sacral) if we desire to be empowered by a positive self-image and inner peace (solar plexus). Subsequently, embodying all these is needed to feel love, connection, and harmony (heart), and to be able to ascend to the higher states of consciousness.

Being willing and open to continually grow and maintain empathetic and harmoneous connection with others (heart) is essential to finding meaning in existence as well as to create with authenticity (throat), to have intuitive clarity and make a difference in the community (third eye), and finally to foster pure awareness and be of service to humanity and the planet (crown).

---

27   Please refer to the third step of P.A.U.S.E. to learn about shadows.

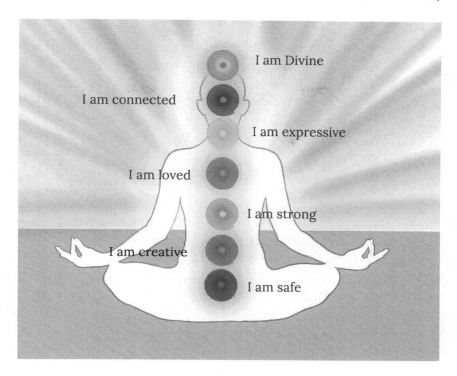

I am Divine

I am connected

I am expressive

I am loved

I am strong

I am creative

I am safe

Ken Wilber, the renowned philosopher and founder of integral theory, has a similar interpretation of developmental stages of consciousness. He proclaims as we evolve, our capacity for *inclusivity* increases from each stage to the next one after the other:

- From egocentric to ethnocentric— from "me" to "us"
- From ethnocentric to worldcentric— from "us" to "all of us"
- From worldcentric to integral— from "all of us" to "all of reality, both manifest and unmanifest"

Unswerving introspection, self-reflection, personal growth, perspective shifting, and cultivation of compassion for oneself and others allow us to gracefully traverse these stages and fulfill our human evolution.

An Indian Hindu sage, Ramana Maharshi, said, "Your own Self-Realization is the greatest service you can render the world." He luminously said the most vital question we must diligently seek to answer is, "Who am I?" Daisaku Ikeda, a Buddhist philosopher, and a nuclear disarmament advocate, similarly emphasized the importance of an individual endeavor for inner realization, "A great human revolution in just a single individual will help achieve a change in the destiny of a nation and, further, can even enable a change in the destiny of all humankind."

Separation is an Illusion

I was born to a country that had gracefully implemented the first democratic government in the history of humankind, and yet its people suffered from injustice, lack of freedom of speech, religion, ideology, and basic human rights many years later. In 539 B.C., Cyrus the Great, the first king of the Persian Empire, freed the slaves and declared religious freedom and racial equality. Cyrus' Cylinder, now kept in the British Museum in London in the United Kingdom, is recognized as the world's first charter of human rights.

Unlike the common trend, knowing this story never inspired me to invest in nationalism but its opposite. Since I was 13, I felt I belonged not to a country but to the entire planet. I actually called myself a cosmopolitan at the age of 14. Even my young heart knew that our values don't come from our past, our beliefs, our status, our possessions, and our achievements. I knew that heavily identifying with any ism or sect could corrupt my soul with pride and ignorance and separate me from the truth of our oneness.

We move through experiences that trigger our untouched memories from the beginning of time to help us learn, discover our divine aspects, and offer them as gifts to the entire creation.

Our isolated bodies, unique genetic dispositions, nuclear families and different cultures, nationalities, beliefs, and biases give us an illusion of separation and we feel lost, alone, scared, and spiritually bankrupt. Because of our myopic vision, we suffer through our human experiences, forgetting that we chose them ourselves.

We blame the people in our inner circle as they push our buttons and drive us insane. We forget that we asked them to push our buttons. It seems William Shakespeare knew this when he said, "All the world's a stage, and all the men and women merely players: they have their exits and their entrances; and one man in his time plays many parts, his acts being seven ages."

When we remember who we are, we can gracefully surpass the façade of our human experiences regardless of their adversity and release ourselves from a victim mentality.

Our human experiences are all geared toward bringing more awareness of our authentic Self, fostering compassion for ourselves and others, and ultimately embodying divine love. By remembering who we truly are and what our mission is, we transcend the events and people's behavior as if we are wearing X-Ray vision goggles. This way we can graciously release our judgments, prejudices, and expectations. We know that this is all a play. Our task is to live our essence, which is limitless divine love and benevolence, and understand separation is an illusion. Thich Nhat Hanh said, "We are here to awaken from our illusion of separateness."

Ins and Outs of Manifestation

When a man saw the Angel of Death looking at him with wrath, he rushed to King Solomon to get him to India to keep him safe. The King bestowed his wish by commanding the wind to take him to the uttermost part of India. Later, when King Solomon asked the Angel of Death why he looked at the man with wrath, he replied, "It was not wrath; it was astonishment. I was supposed to take the man's life in India at that moment and I was wondering how he could get there so quickly!"

Asides from myriads of lessons in this story, Rumi warned us to be watchful of what we desire. Broadening our perspec-tives, deepening our awareness, and being vigilant about our intentions are critical when we desire something. Desires that are ego-driven and self-centered might even bring misery when they are fulfilled. Divine-centered desires that are accompanied by good wishes for others and in hopes of service to the cosmos fulfill us even *while* we are in the process of desiring them.

As humans, we want to be and have more than what we are and have right now. Also, we do not want more—we want it all!

There are basically no limits to our yearning. It's essential to re-wire this tendency if we ever want peace. If we practice living with joy and gratitude even before reaching our goals, we win; if not, we lose. This prevents us from linking our happiness to our desires and wild-goose-chasing something in the future. This way we are no longer at the mercy of conditional happiness, but *we are happy in the moment* regardless of our condition. It's imperative that we take charge of our scarcity mindset and endless impulsive yearning and not let them control us.

Staying connected to our boundlessly compassionate essence assures us that we honor our carefully chosen worldly desires and divine aspirations with wisdom and grace. If we know that we are inherently abundant, capable, deserving, and divinely supported and loved, we get out of our own way. Our only limit is the limit we construct in our mind. Although it sounds intimidating, it's also empowering to know that we are our one and only obstacle in manifesting divine inspiration. Embodying this truth is the alchemy to living the life of our dreams here and now.

Paulo Coelho, in his brilliant book The Alchemist said, "When you want something, all the universe conspires in helping you to achieve it." When your heart desires something, it not only means you deserve it, it means it's already so. Otherwise, you wouldn't even think of it. Be vigilant of your energy. If you feel needy and desperate, you are emitting the energy of lack. Use the phrase, "Wouldn't it be awesome if...?"

The following is a simple manifestation guideline. Use the worksheet to get clear and tell the universe what you are actually seeking. If you don't know, how will the universe know?

Manifestation Exercise

"Stop acting so small. You are the universe in ecstatic motion."
—*Rumi*

1.   Cultivate gratitude for what you already have.

2.   Know exactly what you do not want and what you do want.

3.   Find and release your limiting beliefs.

4. Ask what your heart desires. At the end always append, "... with ease, grace, joy, and ever-increasing peace for myself, my family, and humanity as a collective."
5. For a few seconds every day, allow yourself to radically feel as if you have already achieved your goals.
6. Let go of the result. Trust.

Manifestation Journal

What does my heart desire to have and **when**?
How do I want to **feel** when I achieve them?
What **limiting beliefs** should I **release** that keep me from reaching my goals?

Health: _____

_____

_____

_____

Relationship: _____

_____

_____

_____

Career and finances: _____

_____

_____

_____

Personal development: _____

_____

_____

_____

Last Words

"Mindfulness helps you fall in love with the ordinary."
—Thich Nhat Hanh

A man was passing by a dog that was moaning with pain. He asked the owner about the reason. The owner replied, "He is sitting on a nail." The man astonishingly asked, "Why is he not moving then?" The owner responded, "Because the nail is not hurting him enough!"

There will be a time in our lives that our pain becomes unbearable regardless of how many checkboxes we checked and how many band aids we applied on our inner wounds. This is the tipping point when we have no choice but to move from our comfort zone and reflect on our life on a deeper level.

This is not a moment to mourn or feel ashamed, but a moment for celebration. If something is coming up, it's coming up to leave. This is not a time to label ourselves with disorders and diseases. It's our time for a great awakening, the time to shed our past and learn a new way of living with unconditional joy and peace.

When we learn *The Art of Living in Joy*, we know that nothing and no one has the power to make us happy or unhappy unless we give them the permission to do so. We know that we feel what we feel because we identify with our thoughts and believe our stories and interpretations. We know what we feel in the current moment is a regurgitated experience from the past. Until we P.A.U.S.E. and heal the past, we repeat the emotional pattern.

We know our triggers keep vexing us until we have deconstructed them. We know all our life experiences are here to help us learn our unlearned lessons and that life is an upward spiral of learning, relapsing, and relearning. We know that we don't have control over people and events, but we definitely have control over how we can respond to people and events both internally and externally.

When we look at everyone and every event as a means for our evolution and growth, we become humble students and our life becomes a purposeful school. They are showing us our past wounds and fear-based conditioning. We must thank them and get to work.

Having cognizance of our mind's mechanics and its role in deciphering events is paramount in choosing our responses. Knowing that our lower primitive part of the brain continuously monitors our surrounding for possible threats because it's designed to keep us safe helps us choose which defense program to allow and which to deny. Our main task becomes to perpetually replace our fight-flight-freeze mechanism with our higher brain functions to disrupt fear-based patterns, tap into the wisdom of our heart, find creative solutions, and see opportunities for love and growth.

At the time we are triggered or feel despair and frustration, welcoming each and every feeling and sensation and befriending our inner terrain allows us to live like water, in the flow and emancipated. Research shows even the physical pain diminishes if we transcend victimizing thoughts and completely feel the sensations. By being present with our pains with no judgment, it gracefully comes and leaves.

By practicing mindfulness, we can treasure our current blessings, dismantle our regrets from the past and expectations for the future, and revel in the marvel of our ordinary life to unshackle ourselves from suffering. Whether we believe we have been duped to live in a random and hostile world or reside in a purposeful and benevolent universe, we are equally right because we live what we believe.

Why on earth do we choose fear over love, suffering over peace, and scarcity over abundance, when everything around us and inside us is abundant and graceful?

We have 37.2 trillion cells in our body that function graciously and miraculously all day and all night. We have 100,000s of hair strands on our head and approximately 86 billion neurons in our brain. Earth's beaches contain roughly seven quintillion and five quadrillion grains of sand (7.5 followed by 17 zeros). There are 200 thousand million stars in our own galaxy, the Milky Way. It's estimated that our universe contains at least 70 septillion stars (7 followed by 23 zeros). A big oak tree has around two million leaves. There are 60,065 species of trees on our planet and the natural world contains about 8.7 million species.

I challenge you to find one thing in our world and in nature that is not abundant and limitlessly intelligent. Even in extreme conditions, nature creates abundance. Robert Frost, the renowned American poet said, "Nature is always hinting at us. It hints over and over again. And suddenly we take the hint."

The scope of our prosperity and physical and emotional wellbeing is a reflection of our deep-rooted beliefs and their energetic embodiment. Next time you catch yourself thinking there isn't enough money to go around or you don't deserve to be abundantly wealthy, entirely healthy, and unconditionally joyful, allow nature to be your teacher and let these staggering numbers shatter your limiting beliefs.

The bottom-line is perspectives. Once we know who we truly are, we unchain ourselves from all thoughts that keep us in fear, scarcity, shame, and blame. We gracefully manifest our birthright to feel safe, bountiful, whole, and joyful. Esther Hicks said, "As you think thoughts that feel good to you, you will be in harmony with who you really are. When joy is really important to you, you do not allow yourself to focus upon things that do not feel good—and the result of thinking only thoughts that feel good would cause you to create a wonderful life filled with all things that you desire."

If I weren't born and raised under a tyrannical regime until my early twenties, I wouldn't be able to cherish my freedom every day and not take it for granted. If I hadn't gone through my first abusive marriage, my soul wouldn't have known what kind of a soulmate to seek. If it wasn't for my boss in my last corporate job, I wouldn't have resigned and started my soul-searching journey. If my daughter hadn't given me a hard time, I wouldn't have deepened my understanding of the human condition and wouldn't have found my purpose in life. If I wasn't traumatized by the scamming incident, I wouldn't have learned to truly savor the joy that's deeply embedded in every moment.

We must remember we are the director of our movie and refrain from getting sucked into the everyday narrative, otherwise we lose perspective and become ineffective. We magically have and can access all the knowledge of the universe similar to the way we access the worldwide web through our personal computers or smart phones. We just need to learn how to decipher the information we constantly and graciously receive within ourselves.

Sitting in silence at least twenty minutes a day, self-reflecting, attending to our feelings, questioning our thoughts, activating our heart, and perpetually choosing love over fear are some of the tools that can rewire our brain from incessant mind-wandering and badgering fear-thinking in exchange for increasing harmony and knowingness.

As we use our rational mind as a "faithful servant" and question our adverse thoughts and master our behavior, we increasingly tap into the truth in our heart and contribute to changing our outer world aligned with our values and inner aspirations. We must keep in mind that this is a moment-by-moment endeavor. The journey is the destination. The secret is to witness every moment without judgment and expectation. The more we need to get somewhere, the further we might drift because we are vibrating as if we are not there yet. Energy cannot be fabricated; it needs to be lived.

Release guilt, haste, and perfectionism. Walk the walk to go from the surface to the depth of your soul, from quantity to quality, from uncertainty to stability, and from dependency to freedom. True joy is within our reach at all times, merely one breath away. As long as we fallaciously believe something on the outside can make us happy, we are going nowhere but into a rabbit hole.

The recipe is simple. If a thought or experience brings you joy, keep it; if not, dump it. Also, if a feeling brings you joy, feel it and revel in it; if not, feel it to heal it.

Thoughts lead to feelings, and feelings lead to behavior. All behavior is a form of communication and merely a symptom and we must transcend it to see the underlying unmet needs beneath it.

Let's also remember that all feelings are messengers, and we must attend to them and feel them so they can easily leave our body like the waves of the ocean.

Lastly, let's remember that thoughts stem from our past conditioning. We must become cognizant of them, inspect them, question them, and choose to release them if they are fear-based and disempowering, and believe them if they are inspiring.

As you traverse this journey, recognize that you are rewiring your brain not only from childhood shackles but from generational pain and fear that has been ingrained within your DNA. This is not a job for the faint of heart. Give yourself time, loads of compassion, and plenty of leeway and space to blunder. The desire of not tripping is the biggest obstacle of all.

Every moment we have is a chance for reinventing ourselves anew. When we see ourselves as extraordinary, we create an extraordinary life. Keep reminding yourself that your self-worth doesn't come from your status, your accomplishments, your degree, your bank account, and even your family. You are whole, enough, divinely supported, unconditionally loved, and fully accepted just because you exist. Treat yourself with grace. You deserve it!

Conditional Happiness
vs.
Unconditional Joy

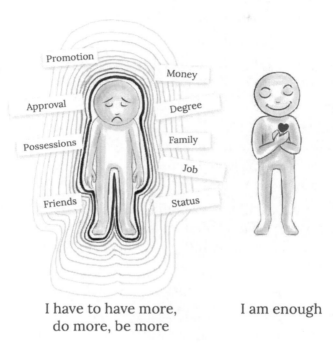

Promotion

Money

Approval

Degree

Possessions

Family

Job

Friends

Status

I have to have more,
do more, be more

I am enough

Heart Exercise

Even if we are exposed to the most transformational knowledge, unless we *act* upon the information, it will be just a nice addition to our bookshelf—in this case, literally. Please do this last exercise regularly to unshackle from the suffering of the mind, embody joy and freedom, and transport yourself to the higher planes of consciousness.

Our ultimate task is to cultivate awareness of our mental and emotional states and revel in them if they contain love, peace, and joy, and if not, shift them by taking a P.A.U.S.E. and using our tools. An evolved life is always about shifting from fear in our mind to the love in our heart and knowing that our essence is of love, compassion, abundance, and joy. If we want to create an amazing life, we must first feel amazing within ourselves.

1. Set at least three daily reminders on your phone.

2. When the alarm goes off, relax the muscles on your forehead, close your eyes, drop your shoulders, and put a *smile* on your face.

3. Take three deep breaths to your heart. Breathe in deep through your nose and breathe out long from your mouth. With each breath, imagine a wave of relaxation from the top of your head to your toes.

4. Take your one-minute mindful breathing microbreak by detaching from your thoughts and paying attention to the sensation of your breathing on your chest or under your nostrils.[28]

5. Put your hands on your heart and think of three things you are grateful for. Feel deep gratitude for them.

6. Rate yourself from 0 to 10 – 10 being the most joyful, peaceful, and abundant.

7. If you are not at 10, P.A.U.S.E. [29] and then use the power of your mind to pull yourself up to 10.

8. When you are at 10, put your hands on your heart, use a mantra or a word that describes this state, and truly feel your euphoric feelings for at least 10 seconds.

---

28   Please check the first step of P.A.U.S.E.
29   P.A.U.S.E.: Pause and breathe. Accept the as-is and feel your feelings. Understand thoughts and triggers. Search for a different perspective. Eliminate fear and find win-win solutions with love and compassionate boundaries.

9. I magine yourself at a time and space where all your aspirations and desires have already come true. Revel in the feeling fort another 10 seconds.
10. Get up and dance like no one is watching!

> *"For years my heart inquired of me*
> *Where the Divine Chalice might be,*
> *And what was in its own possession*
> *It asked from strangers, constantly."*
> *– Hafez*

My Notes and Commitments

My biggest takeaways:

_____

_____

_____

_____

_____

_____

What do I commit to do **every day** to empower myself to P.A.U.S.E.: (E.g.: mindful living, questioning my thoughts, radical self-acceptance, self-care, choosing love and joy over fear and scarcity-mindset on a moment-to-moment basis,...)?

_____

_____

_____

_____

_____

_____

Ancient Nahuatl Blessing

I release my parents from the feeling that they have already failed me.

I release my children from the need to bring pride to me; that they may write their own ways according to their hearts that whisper all the time in their ears.

I release my partner from the obligation to complete myself. I do not lack anything; I learn with all beings all the time.

I thank my grandparents and forefathers who have gathered so that I can breathe life today.

I release them from past failures and unfulfilled desires, aware that they have done their best to resolve their situations within the consciousness they had at that moment.

I honor you, I love you, and I recognize you as innocent.

I am transparent before your eyes, so they know that I do not hide or owe anything other than being true to myself and to my very existence; that walking with the wisdom of the heart, I am aware that I fulfill my life purpose, free from invisible and visible family loyalties that might disturb my peace and happiness, which are my only responsibilities.

I renounce the role of savior, of being one who unites or fulfills the expectations of others.

Learning through and only through love, I bless my essence, my way of expressing, even though somebody may not understand me.

I understand myself, because I alone have lived and experienced my history; because I know myself, I know who I am, what I feel, what I do and why I do it.

I respect and approve of myself.

I honor the divinity in me and in you.
We are free.

Conscious Living Manifesto

I take care of myself on a daily basis by meditating, walking in nature, eating wholesome foods, and releasing negative self-talk, expectations, resentment, control, and fear. I know **self-care** is not selfish; it's necessary. I give from the overflow of my energy.

I attempt to fill up my unmet needs of **connectedness, competence,** and **autonomy** on a daily basis. If I have a child, I will try to fulfill theirs too.

I know people have been called forth to show me where I can **heal** and **grow myself** authentically and fully.

I try to regularly P.A.U.S.E. to reprogram my brain **from fear to love**.

When I get triggered, I make an attempt **P.A.U.S.E.:**

Pause and breath: I separate myself physically or emotionally as soon as I get triggered by using my mantra, connecting to my body and taking deep breaths. I avoid fighting, arguing, or fixing on the spot.

Accept the as-is and feel feelings: I accept the reality of the situation, feel my feelings for at least 20 seconds, and attend to my inner child.

Understand thoughts and triggers: I understand that the current situation pokes a past wound in me, and it is best to take care of myself to prevent projecting my fears onto the present moment. I ask myself, "What do I need at this time?"

Search for a different perspective: I know "misbehavior" is a symptom and a sign of unmet needs. I know hurt people hurt people. I know everything happens for me, not to me. I try to focus on how I can heal and evolve through my experiences.

Eliminate fear and find win-win solutions with love and compassionate boundaries: I know I am responsible for enforcing my personal boundaries, not others, and I do that with calmness, clarity, and compassion. I do not say no when I want to say yes, or say yes when I want to say no.

I forgive myself as soon as I am aware of my unconsciousness and P.A.U.S.E. to repair and learn. I know that brain rewiring is a journey, not a destination.

Name, date, and signature:

The Art of Living in Joy

PROGRAMS

Personal Healing

Conscious Relationships

Conscious Parenting

Goal-Setting

Private Sessions

Group Coaching

Corporate Training

To learn more about the programs and how I might be of service to you, book a free call at:

DRARAYEH.COM

Made in the USA
Middletown, DE
30 December 2022

20810935R00146